BETWEEN THE LINES

BETWEEN THE LINES

A MEMOIR ABOUT ADDICTION, EMPATHY, AND EVOLUTION

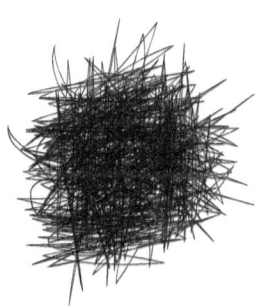

JAY LIND

COPYRIGHT © 2022 JAY LIND
All rights reserved.

BETWEEN THE LINES
A Memoir about Addiction, Empathy, and Evolution

ISBN   978-1-5445-2799-4 *Hardcover*
           978-1-5445-2798-7 *Paperback*
           978-1-5445-2800-7 *Ebook*

For my mom and dad,
And for my sons.

CONTENTS

Introduction IX

My Dad 1
Dr. A: My Therapist 7
Randy: A Friend 15
Chris: My Brother 25
Wayne: A Drug Addict 33
David: A Drug Addict 41
Bradley: An Alcoholic 45
An Eighteen-Year-Old Boy in a Cook County Jail Cell 51
Glenn: A Friend 57
Daisy: An Alcoholic 63
Kyle: A Drug Addict 69
Jake and Henry: A Drug Addict and His Little Brother 75

A Letter to the Loved Ones of Addicts
and Alcoholics Everywhere   81
Anne Piaccini: An Assistant State's Attorney   91
Carl Mason: My Probation Officer   99
My Dad   107
Scott: A Sex Offender Therapist   113
Grace: A Polygraph Administrator   129
C.J.: A Sex Offender   135
Brent: A Sex Offender   141
Kathy: A Friend's Mom   147
Mary Beth: Teacher, Mentor, Another Friend's Mom   151
Max: A Friend and Mary Beth's Son   159
Book Club   175
Dana: My Ex-Wife   183
Jasper and Rocket: My Kids   191
My Mom   203
Jessa: My Former Student, My Victim   209
My Dad   223
Epilogue: Jessa: A Survivor, My Partner   231

Acknowledgments   243

INTRODUCTION

Near the top of the rather lengthy list of concerns I had as I sat down to start writing this book about four years ago was my fear that the end product would be thought of as some kind of list of excuses for the mistakes I have made as a father, husband, brother, son, friend, or teacher. Or even worse, that my words would be misconstrued as some sort of denial of any wrongdoing or even an attempt to minimize the colossal damage left in the wake of my actions. So, let me say it right at the top: I take full responsibility for the monumental mistakes I've made in my life, most importantly for my regrettable actions in the fall of 2015. I am solely responsible for the reckless decisions I made and for all of the undeniable sadness, anxiety, and pain that I caused to the people and communities I care about the most. When 2015 began, I was happily married with two perfect sons. We had recently moved into a house just down the street from my childhood home. I was a successful and well-regarded English teacher in the high school that my brother, sister, and I all graduated from.

I really did have it all, and not in some kind of superficial way. I was living my dream in the truest sense. And I was feeling good about what I had made of myself and what I was doing with my life. I was making a difference in the best kind of way, and I was happy. But I risked it all by engaging in inappropriate and illegal sexual contact with one of my former students during her senior year of high school. I don't believe any good would come from me writing anything else about the specific details of my offense. And I don't intend to do that in this book. But what the local media reported about it at the time was generally accurate. I've never denied it to anyone. And I won't do it here.

I did it. And I will never stop being remorseful or sorry for what I did. The guilt I feel as a result of my actions during that period of my life doesn't weigh on me the way it used to, but I will never forget it or truly forgive myself for hurting so many people.

INTRODUCTION

So much has happened in the years that have passed since I walked out of my old school for the last time. I was charged with several felonies as a result of my actions that fall, and I was subsequently convicted of one count of aggravated criminal sexual abuse. If convicted on all the charges against me, I was facing decades in the state penitentiary. But thanks to my family, friends, colleagues, and privilege, I was spared any time in prison. In the end, I was sentenced to two years of sex offender probation and ordered to complete eighteen months of intensive sex offender therapy. I lost my job and my teaching license. And after months of counseling, my wife and I decided that our marriage was over as well. Thankfully, my ex-wife and I have remained close, and we work very well together, co-parenting our two sons.

My dad passed away about a year before I unraveled and dismantled the life and career I had spent so much time and energy building. And my dad was my hero. He battled brain cancer for about a year before he eventually died in bed at our family farm, surrounded by all the people who cared about him the most. I loved my dad very much, and losing him was devastating in a million ways. And my general coping mechanisms for dealing with that loss can only be described as dangerous and unhealthy. Most notable of my many unhealthy coping mechanisms and strategies to process my grief was my abuse of drugs and alcohol. What began as a temporary escape ended up being my demise. As it turns out, to nobody's surprise, I am a drug addict. And there is no other way to say that.

When my dad got sick, I let my addiction take hold of my entire life. And I never asked for help. I guess I had to hit the proverbial rock bottom that everyone talks about. This is at least part of the reason why it has taken me years to process and eventually accept my dad's death. I miss him just as much today as I did the day he died, and I will never stop grieving for him, but that is part of the human experience. And I am grateful for that. I am in a much better place with my sadness today because I have finally learned how to grieve for him and miss him in a healthy and appropriate way. I am no longer trying to get over it. I'm just trying to find a healthy way to carry it with me forever. And after countless hours of therapy and pages and pages of reading and writing, I have come to find great value in what my dad taught me while he was alive. In many ways, it has been those very life lessons that have guided me through my personal journey to recovery from my addiction and, eventually, to making amends with the people I have hurt.

My dad's learned willingness to own his mistakes and flaws, along with his ability to examine those mistakes and to use them to become a better man, may be two of the most

INTRODUCTION

valuable lessons I've ever learned. But along with his painful but useful self-awareness, my dad also passed on to me his desire to collect the stories of everyone around him and learn from those stories in the same way he learned from his own experience. My dad taught me to look for myself in every person I meet. These inherited character traits serve as the inspiration and backbone of *Between the Lines*. And while my dad's illness and eventual death were the catalysts for what proved to be a devastating and destructive downward spiral for me, what he taught me while he was alive was, and continues to be, an integral factor in my continued recovery and evolution as a human being. Sometimes, the worst thing that ever happened to you is also the best thing that ever happened to you.

Between the Lines is, in part, my story of addiction, relapse, and continuing recovery. On a different level, it's about my experience in Cook County's criminal justice system as a very privileged, straight White man—a man born with any and all of the advantages needed to live a happy and successful life. I cannot deny that I belong to that small subgroup of Americans born on third base. And if you've ever seen me run, you'd know I sure as shit didn't hit a triple. But as I approach fifty years of age, I'm still trying to find my way to home plate without leaving the basepath or tripping over my own ignorance.

On yet another level, *Between the Lines* is a retelling of my experience in sex offender therapy and as a father who will most likely remain on the sex offender registry for the rest of my life. But it's also the story of the extraordinary mistakes I made and the damage and pain they left behind. And, to a lesser extent, *Between the Lines* is about my very public fall from grace in the community where I grew up and where my family and nearly all of my friends still live.

Each chapter of *Between the Lines* gets its title from a person or group of people who have played important roles in my story. I have known some of these people for my whole life, but some of the others are people I would've never known if I hadn't fallen so far and so hard in the years surrounding my dad's death. Some of these important people went out of their way to look after me, hold me up, and encourage me when it would have been understandable and probably easier to let me sit in my own mess until I figured out how to clean it up myself. But the undeniable truth is that I couldn't have found the renewed happiness and purpose that I have in my life today without the love and support of these extraordinary people. Most likely, I wouldn't have survived much past my first court date without their help. These people quite literally saved my life, or at the very least, allowed me to save my own life.

INTRODUCTION

Some of the other people featured in the chapters of *Between the Lines* taught me some essential truths and helped me evolve simply by trusting me with their stories. It is my sincerest hope that sharing my story with them had a similar impact on their lives. Anyone who chooses to read *Between the Lines* will learn about my journey in bits and pieces as they take in the stories of some of the significant and unique people I've encountered along the way. So it could be said that *Between the Lines* isn't really about me at all. It's about everyone else and the perspective I've gained by listening to their stories...and learning from them. I really do consider it a gift. And I feel obligated to pay it forward.

Between the Lines is a memoir, albeit a memoir with a slightly unconventional structure. And to respect the privacy and confidentiality of the people whose stories I've included in the following chapters, I used pseudonyms and changed other identifying details when necessary. The last thing I want to do is hurt or re-traumatize anyone involved. That would be the exact opposite of what I've always hoped to accomplish with this book. *Between the Lines* is meant to be an act of empathy, compassion, and understanding, and that applies to each and every person whose story appears in the following chapters, along with anyone who chooses to read them. I consider writing this book to be part of the ninth step of my recovery. In more ways than one, this is only the beginning of what I plan on doing to make living amends for the undeniable and unnecessary pain that I've caused over the years.

My mission in writing *Between the Lines* was clear to me when I scribbled the first words of it into my journal during a group therapy session in one of my multiple stints in a drug abuse rehabilitation facility. And I'm confident that it will be worth it. There is a saying about smooth seas not making strong sailors, and I couldn't agree more. When I encountered dangerous waters for the first time in my life, after forty years of clear sailing, I just curled up below deck and hoped that the storm would pass. Instead, I was thrown overboard, and I nearly died. My experience treading water and doing my best to stay afloat over the last seven years has given me a truly unique perspective on life, a perspective that I surely wouldn't have gained had the seas remained smooth for the rest of my life. The mistakes I made at sea and the consequences that I faced as a result left me with a newfound perspective and an ability to shed some light where light desperately needs to be shed. And that is precisely what I set out to do when I put pen to paper and started writing *Between the Lines*.

Grief and loss are human and universal, and there aren't any silver bullets for dealing with them, but if sharing my experience can help even one person cope with the loss of a

INTRODUCTION

loved one, it will be more than worth it. And sadly, addiction and alcoholism also affect the lives of just about everyone on the planet in one way or another. If you are lucky enough not to have the disease, then chances are someone close to you does. And the impact that addiction and alcoholism have on our loved ones can be just as serious as the impact on the addict or alcoholic. It's like cancer that way. Writing *Between the Lines* has been key to my recovery, and it will be one of my greatest accomplishments in life if what I have written in these pages provides even a sliver of hope to someone suffering under the strong thumb of addiction, be that an addict or anyone who loves one. A little hope goes a long way.

I decided on *Between the Lines* as the title for my memoir just a few short days after I came up with the idea for its content and structure. It occurred to me then that the title could work on a few different levels. And keeping it in mind has guided me in my writing. It has served as a constant reminder of my original mission. In one way, the title is my announcement to the reader that *my* story exists between the lines of the other stories I tell in the book. But the "lines" in the title also allude to the moral and legal boundaries I've had a problem abiding by throughout my life. Lastly, cocaine was my drug of choice, the drug that dominated my thoughts, feelings, and behavior for so many years. But the uncountable lines of cocaine I snorted during those years are only part of what happened back then. How I felt and what I did between those lines are at the core of my story. I do have to say, though, that I have been worried from the start that people might see *Between the Lines* on a bookshelf somewhere and think that it's some kind of driver's education textbook, or a book about football, or maybe even one of those new adult coloring books. But I was willing to take that risk. And, in the end, I'm glad I did.

For almost as long as I can remember, I've had a sometimes debilitating fear of being exposed. My dean in high school once told me that I should always act as if my mom was secretly watching my every move. I remember thinking how horrible that would be if everything I was doing back then was suddenly brought into the light, *especially* if my mom could see it. This fear of being exposed probably doesn't haunt the average person how it haunted me for so long. But what I have learned through all of this is that my fear of being exposed in high school came from a very real place. It was almost solely based on the fact that the way I was living my life didn't match up with the core values I believed in. It was an issue of personal integrity...an issue much more common with the rebellious teenager than the fortysomething, suburban high school teacher.

INTRODUCTION

Most people, I believe, gain integrity with age. And there is no doubt that I was headed in the right direction for some time, beginning in my early twenties. And as my family relationships got stronger and I became more entrenched and self-confident in my career as a teacher, I was beginning to feel truly proud of who I had become. Maybe I had learned from my youthful mistakes. But in time, the familiar feelings of guilt and shame returned, and so did my fear of being exposed.

Roughly twenty-five years after my dean gave me that sage advice in his office, I was teaching in that very same school when I started one of my freshmen classes with a journal prompt. I'd used this particular prompt several times over the years, and it was always one of my favorites. I wrote the question on the board, "What do you fear?" We all wrote for five or ten minutes before I asked if anyone wanted to share. After a few of my students shared some of their fears with the class, one of them asked me what I wrote about. I told them that I wrote about my fear of being exposed. I remember that I had a hard time explaining it to them. And I thought about that from time to time over the next year or two, and I finally made some sense of it. The gap between my behavior and my core values was widening again.

One might think that writing a memoir and sharing it with anyone willing to read it probably isn't the wisest decision for a person who fears exposure more than just about anything else in the world. And they could be right. There is no doubt that as much as I believe in the mission that inspired and motivated me to write *Between the Lines*, I am also feeling more and more uncomfortable and anxious as it gets closer to becoming a real, on-the-shelf book. During my fifteen years in the classroom, I would often remind my students that when they felt uncomfortable or anxious about an assignment or a class discussion, they were probably getting ready to learn something. "Lean into the discomfort," I would tell them. Well, I guess *Between the Lines* is my chance to see how closely my actions match my core values today.

MY DAD

I summoned my dad into my room one night when I was maybe fifteen years old. I wanted him to listen to a song I liked. This practice of trying to convince my dad that there was indeed some music worth listening to that was created after Buddy Holly's death would continue right up until the year he died. In fact, we spent most of 2003 engaged in an ongoing and sometimes heated debate regarding the artistic and cultural value of hip-hop music. But the song I was introducing him to on that particular night was almost universally acclaimed. I figured it would be an easy sell and that maybe it could bring my dad and me one step closer to finding some common ground.

"Man in the Mirror" was the song, and at that time, the full extent of Michael Jackson's personal struggle, as well as the majority of his controversial behavior, hadn't yet been made public. So, when my dad reluctantly stepped into my room that night, I immediately pumped up the volume on the oversized boom box I was clutching on my lap. And I watched his reaction carefully as the King of Pop sang to us both. The verse I played for him had a pretty clear message that I wasn't quite internalizing at the time, but it was one that was obviously relevant to my behavior and attitude at that stage of my adolescence.

I was looking in the mirror for all the wrong reasons back then, usually just to check my hair. It must've been clear to my dad that I was missing the metaphor because he just smiled and slowly pivoted away from me, apparently choosing to leave my room without offering any kind of analysis or opinion on the song. But I paused the cassette long enough to stop him and ask him what he thought. Without even turning around or breaking his stride, he suggested, in a tone that can only be described as mildly dismissive, that maybe I should listen to the lyrics.

MY DAD

A few years later, in the fall of my senior year in high school, my dad accidentally overheard a phone conversation I was having with my girlfriend, Melissa. It was a few days after the homecoming dance, and Melissa, who earned the unfortunate honor of being my date that night, had a few not-so-nice things to say about the way I behaved at the hotel party we attended after the dance. She was letting me know, in not-so-gentle terms, how disrespectful, unacceptable, and disgusting it was of me and some of the other guys who were there to make fun of, demean, and flat-out bully one of the girls at the party...a girl who clearly drank too much, too fast.

I still remember this conversation with Melissa and how it made me feel as if I had just now returned the clunky phone to the cradle mounted on the wall of my childhood bedroom. I was embarrassed and ashamed of my behavior, as I often was those days. But, as usual, I was unwilling and unable to look in the mirror and acknowledge any of the very real mistakes I'd made. The guilt and shame I felt back then were sometimes crippling. So, as was the case whenever I was confronted about my behavior, I fell back on my pitiful routine of denial and excuse-making. My half-assed apology on the phone that day was more of a declaration that I wasn't really responsible for my behavior on homecoming night, on account of my obvious drunkenness. But unbeknownst to me, my dad was standing in the hall just outside of my room, and he heard every word of this feeble attempt to avoid being held accountable for my actions.

After Melissa was done giving me a much-deserved piece of her mind, then rightfully refusing to let me off the hook for what I had done, my dad walked into my room and sat down next to me on my bed. This always meant that it was time for us to have a little man-to-man conversation. We sat side by side on the edge of my bed and talked pretty regularly during that stage of my increasingly problematic adolescence. But that night, after he had finished listening to me making cowardly and weak excuses to Melissa, we didn't have much of a conversation at all.

On this particular occasion, my dad did all of the talking. And his message was clear. He told me not to use being drunk as an excuse for my bad behavior. I got drunk, he reminded me, and that decision was all mine. Therefore, the consequences were all mine too. I needed to accept that fact and learn from the experience. If I refused to face that difficult truth, then I was bound to make the same mistakes again and again, and the consequences would only get worse. And my dad didn't want that for me. After each and every one of our man-to-man sit-downs, he made sure to tell me how much he loved me before leaving me in my room to consider everything he'd said. That night was no exception. Melissa broke up with me a couple of days later. And although I continued to get drunk and make bad decisions for approximately twenty-five more years, I never used "I was drunk" as an excuse again.

My dad was always sympathetic and understanding, but he didn't mince his words. Whenever he gave me advice, he started by reminding me that he only felt comfortable and qualified to advise me on such matters because he had made many of the same mistakes in his life. Sometimes he told me what those mistakes were, but usually, he just made it clear that he had been there. As it turns out, most of my dad's fatherly wisdom was built on and supported by a fairly impressive and diverse portfolio of impulsive behavior and bad decisions that often left him saddled with the same brand of guilt and shame that I felt. But at some point in my dad's life, he started to look in the mirror a little more often. And he finally began learning from his mistakes, and making changes, and evolving. He desperately wanted me to see the benefit of this practice of self-reflection earlier in my life than he did, and even though that wouldn't happen, I will always appreciate how hard he tried to pass it on.

I love my dad, at least in part because of his weaknesses. He was flawed like I am. He told me about it, and he tried to help me learn from the mistakes he'd made. And although I still made many of those same mistakes, along with a few doozies of my own, I did manage to learn some truly valuable lessons from my dad, and I think of him every time I sit down with either of my sons to have a little man-to-man conversation. And I always tell them that I love them before I leave the room.

It took more than forty years for me to fully internalize what my dad spent so much time and energy modeling for me, but there is no doubt that it has become an integral part of who I am today. As a direct result of my dad's thoughtful parenting and painstaking efforts to get better with age, I now know that a real man owns his weaknesses, and his mistakes, and the hurt he has caused. He wears his flaws like scars on his heart. He heals, and he learns, and he never stops evolving. He doesn't want to cause any harm to anyone, especially to the people he loves the most. He makes it his mission to know everyone's story and make a difference in the lives of others. And after leaving an indelible mark of compassion, wit, and wisdom on his family and almost everyone he encounters in his life, he dies at home with a whole heart and a clear conscience, surrounded only by love.

DR. A
MY THERAPIST

There is no doubt that denial is an important roadblock for addicts, especially in the early stages of their addiction. But I'd been through a twelve-step program for compulsive gambling ten years before any of this, and I was well aware of the undeniable and devastating symptoms of addiction. I would deny it to anyone else, of course, but deep inside, I knew I was killing myself. I had known that for some time. I knew I was an addict and that I couldn't get better without help. I was almost forty years old, and my dad was dying. Things were getting really bad for the first time in my life.

I had begun using cocaine before work, at work, and at home when my family was asleep. And I was getting almost no sleep at all. I was pilfering money from the joint account that my wife and I shared, and I was taking countless payday loans in order to fund my frequent binges and benders. And on top of that, I always seemed to owe my dealer hundreds of dollars. And as I felt the walls closing in on me, I only doubled down.

If you didn't know better, you'd think I was trying to kill myself in some kind of spectacular fashion. But right up to the very end, I could've just asked for help. People would've jumped at the chance to save my life. I knew this, and as much as I wanted to get better, nothing could get me to just say the words, "I need help."

This is what separates us from the "normies," as addicts commonly refer to non-addicts in the recovery community; normies are capable of changing their behavior when they notice that, time after time, it ends up resulting in the same negative consequences...especially when those consequences keep getting more and more severe. But without exception, a drug addict reaches rock bottom because, in the face of devastating consequences, and regardless of how hard he tries to stop, he only increases the frequency and intensity of his drug use. There isn't an addict or alcoholic in any AA or NA meeting who didn't first try everything in their power to stop on their own. None of us want to drink or use drugs anymore. We have been trying to quit for years, but we are powerless. Most of us had been stuck on step one for a long time before we ever went to a meeting or checked into a treatment program.

About a year and a half before the climax of my monumental and public self-destruction, there was a brief period of time when I had the tiniest sliver of hope. During a rare moment of clarity and urgency, I hatched a plan that just might have saved me from the storm. I knew I couldn't bring myself to admit my addiction publicly and ask for help, but maybe I could come clean to a therapist I trusted, and they could help rescue me from what was becoming more and more inevitable.

Eventually, I decided to reach out to some friends and ask if any of them had recommendations for a good therapist in the neighborhood. I needed to find someone capable of working miracles with the human spirit. And I found the right man. But initially, I wasn't able or willing to open the door wide enough to let him all the way in. He couldn't save me from the storm that was brewing, but there is no way in hell that I would've survived it, rebuilt my life, and found purpose and happiness again without Dr. A's support and guidance.

Two of my closest friends recommended Dr. A to me. One of those friends had recently gotten through a difficult divorce and a drastic career change with Dr. A's help. The other friend suffered one of the most difficult losses anyone could possibly imagine: his young wife died giving birth to their second child. But with Dr. A's support and gentle guidance, my friend eventually found his footing again. He is now happily married to a wonderful woman, and they have one of the strongest, healthiest, and happiest families I have ever known. I figured that if Dr. A could help these two friends of mine through the significant trauma in their lives, then he was the man I was looking for.

I finally called and made an appointment to see Dr. A. All I needed to do was show up and be honest. And I did just that… for the most part. During my first appointment, at least.

I can recall my first meeting with Dr. A vividly. I remember how the change spilled out of my pockets and into the deep leather couch when I sat down across from him. I remember thinking that he looked kind of like a young Henry Kissinger. But mostly, I remember feeling instantly comfortable in Dr. A's presence.

He opened by asking me what prompted me to call his office for an appointment. I was ready for this question. I even practiced it in the car before I came in. I told him that my

DR. A

dad had been diagnosed with a brain tumor a few months earlier and that I had become increasingly worried about my unhealthy coping mechanisms. I told him I was routinely escaping by drinking and using drugs and that I had a history of compulsive gambling that landed me in a twelve-step program years earlier. He asked a few follow-up questions about the drinking and drug use, and, of course, I then minimized it, but it felt like a good start. And I remember being proud of myself for telling the truth, even if I was leaving out some of the most important details.

I had finally come clean (kind of) and asked for help. We spent the rest of that first meeting talking about my relationship with my dad and my teaching career...my two favorite topics of conversation. When I left Dr. A's office that day, I was skipping steps in the stairwell leading out of the building. I felt like this was the beginning of my road back to a healthy and happy life.

I have continued to see Dr. A about once a week ever since. Our relationship spans over seven years now. But I would do anything to go back in time, to that first year, and tell him the whole truth, mostly about my drug use and my growing and very active addiction to cocaine. I have no doubt that Dr. A would've found a way to get me through the doors of rehab well before my brother took me to Minnesota and checked me in. By that time, the majority of the damage had been done.

Looking back, it's hard to imagine how different things would've been for me if I'd gotten help sooner. But it is a firm belief of mine that had I come clean and asked for help sooner, there is no guarantee that my life would be any better than it is today. It's impossible to say, and playing "what if?" over and over in my head never leaves me feeling very good. At the same time, there are a few things that I know wouldn't have happened. And that would have saved an immeasurable amount of anxiety, fear, and sadness for countless people in my life, most notably, the people who I love more than anything else. But over time, I'm learning to look back less and to refocus my attention to the present. That has made my life much easier to live, and it's one of the many things I have Dr. A to thank for.

There is no doubt in my mind that Dr. A's presence in my life has been a boon greater than almost any other that I've been lucky enough to receive. I'm not sure if he knows this, but even though it has been a mere one hour a week for seven years, Dr. A has been a kind of replacement father figure to me. And keep in mind that my real dad was my hero. Those are some tough loafers to fill.

I often imagine my relationship with Dr. A like the one Michael Jordan had with his bodyguard after Jordan's father

DR. A

was murdered on the side of a North Carolina highway. What I like most about that analogy is that I just compared myself to Michael Jordan. And I thought this might be my only chance to get that in writing.

Dr. A probably didn't know he was even in the running for the job as my new part-time father figure, but I have my suspicions that he realizes now that I consider him to be more than just my therapist. And there are several examples, all of which will stay with me forever, of how Dr. A went above and beyond what anyone would expect from their therapist. First of all, he has always known how precarious my financial situation has been, and as soon as I lost my teaching job and health insurance, the treatment I received from Dr. A became an out-of-pocket expense that I couldn't afford. But it never became an issue, and my weekly appointments continued without interruption.

Initially, Dr. A lowered his hourly rate for me without even mentioning it. But more important than that, he never once pushed me for a payment, even though sometimes I'd go almost a year without finding any money for him. On more than one occasion, Dr. A would casually slip me a twenty on my way out of his office and tell me he wanted to treat me to a coffee or something to eat. And I usually cried all the way home when he did this. There were other times when Dr. A would pay me to do work for him, even though I was rarely paying him for the very important work he was doing for me. I painted his office, cleaned out the attic, picked weeds, planted flowers, and sometimes checked on the building when he wasn't around. He once hired me to paint the shutters on the windows of his house. He wasn't home on the days when I showed up to paint, but I remember nervously knocking on the door before hugging his wife a little harder than I should have. I had never met her before, but she felt like part of my family in a way.

I have a distinct memory of the day I helped Dr. A take a broken air conditioner out to the alley after one of our meetings. Both of us were laughing and sweating profusely as we struggled to get the old machine down the stairs and out the door. And as we set it down next to the garbage cans and smiled at each other, I remember thinking, *This is the kind of thing I'd do with my dad if he were still alive, and this is probably how it would feel.*

RANDY
A FRIEND

Randy was a close friend of mine for many years. We haven't seen each other for quite some time now, but it would be fair to say that I will always consider him a friend. I came to know Randy by way of some connections I made when I was running around in what used to be my secret life. That means that, by design, none of my family, close friends, or colleagues knew much about him at all. And, because the thought of my two lives accidentally colliding frightened me to no end, I did everything in my power to keep it like that.

About a year after I first met Randy, he became something like a partner in crime, although neither of us thought about it like that back then. We would spend hours and hours in his perpetually dark apartment snorting cocaine, smoking cigarettes, playing video ping pong (yes, you read that right), drinking, laughing, scratching lottery tickets, and watching game shows.

What started as an unhealthy but only occasional escape from any issues I was having in the real world eventually became something much more problematic and dangerous. And as I approached rock bottom, Randy was the only one who had any idea how much cocaine I was really doing, but he never knew what all that cocaine was doing to me. I was damn good at hiding any negative impact my drug use was having on my everyday life, even from Randy. That's how bad it got. I was even keeping secrets from the people in my secret life. Keeping up with all of my lies was difficult and sometimes hard to keep track of. And I certainly didn't feel good about it.

The lying really ballooned a few months after the cancer in my dad's brain revealed itself in spectacular fashion. It was never easy for me and getting away with it didn't give me any pleasure, but like so many addicts and alcoholics, I seemed to

RANDY

have a real knack for the art of deception. So, when I knocked on the back door of Randy's apartment at any hour of the day or night, I always managed to come up with some believable story and to put on my happy face by the time he finished his smoke and got up to let me in. He didn't like it when I showed up unannounced, but I found it easier to fly under the radar if my arrival was a surprise to him.

There is no doubt in my mind that had Randy known what was really going on in my head and in my life back then, he would've stopped answering the door months before I checked into rehab for the first time. He wouldn't have wanted any part of what I was doing to myself. And I knew that, so I tried very hard to keep it from him. And although the time I spent sitting on Randy's couch turned out to be part of the darkest years of my life, I do cherish some of the memories I managed to hold on to. The stories I heard, the people I met, and the perspective I gained during that time of my life will remain with me forever. I mean it.

Here's something I can't help but remember. There was this thing Randy would say whenever he felt the need to express how unfairly he was being treated. After going into great detail about the inarguable shittiness of the situation at hand, he would always add a little emphasis to his story by saying to anyone and everyone within earshot, "Now you see what I'm dealing with." He used this particular statement quite often, and it had a very specific purpose. It was meant to remind all of us how difficult and miserable his life had become, even for a minute, as a direct result of some sacrifice he made or some favor he did for some friend in need. It was his own unique spin on the more common "no good deed goes unpunished." It may have been some kind of defense mechanism, or maybe even an attempt to rationalize some of his other not-so-benevolent actions. But I think it mostly served as a reminder to all of us, and himself, that Randy was a good and loyal friend.

There is something I should make clear about Randy (and I'm trying to say this in a way that won't make him want to stop by my place and straighten me out a little). Rarely is he the kindest, gentlest person in the room. I think he'd be the first to admit his occasional issues with anger and rage. And it is no secret that he and I had some conflicting opinions on what I would consider to be America's most significant political and societal issues. In fact, on more than one occasion, after a particularly heated and probably nonsensical debate, I stormed out of Randy's apartment, only to spend the next few days flooding his inbox with old census data and *HuffPost* articles about racial equity and socialized medicine. Randy rarely made reference to any of the material I passed on to him, but I'm sure he read every word. But even if he gave me

RANDY

a fake email address or never read any of the articles I sent, I know in my heart that Randy is a good man, a man with a story far deeper and more complex than it may appear on the surface. And with a little distance between us, it is easier for me to see that we have a lot more in common than either of us would like to admit.

Randy loved talking about his dad. Many of the stories that he recounted for his usually polite and sometimes captive audiences were about his dad's unconventional parenting style. Each of his anecdotes followed the same formula. He always opened with a long and detailed description of how ruthless, stubborn, and harsh his dad could be. It was important to Randy that we all had a clear understanding of the physical, mental, and emotional torment he was forced to endure at the hands of his father. Anyone listening to one of these stories for the first time would think that what they were hearing was surely building up to an outright condemnation of the unfair and ineffective parenting style practiced by Randy's dad...a slightly adjusted version of his "now you see what I'm dealing with" declarations. But, without exception, Randy concluded each story by letting his flock of huddled chain-smokers know, in no uncertain terms, that his dad and his dad's distinctive brand of parenting taught Randy how to change the oil in his car, file his taxes, rake the lawn, improve his credit score, make an open-field tackle, and, above all things, be a man. But Randy never stopped at that.

Despite the fact that Randy didn't have any kids of his own, unlike many of the members of his living-room congregation, he was never shy about dishing out some pro-tips on parenting. Whatever he lacked in experience, he more than made up for in the sheer confidence of his delivery. Randy made sure that every one of the teeth-grinding zombies packed into his dark and smokey living room that day knew, in no uncertain terms, that the way his dad raised him was, in fact, the only effective way to raise a child. I remember laughing (never out loud, of course) at how wholeheartedly Randy endorsed the manner in which he was raised. But the funny thing is, I felt just as strongly about how my parents chose to raise me. And I can assure you that my mom and dad had a parenting style quite contrary to the one Randy was always preaching about.

Essentially, the two very different childhoods that Randy and I spent so much time bragging about were like photo negatives of each other. *But both of us turned out pretty great*, I used to think to myself. Then I'd pull out another cigarette from my pack, not even a minute after I pressed the last one into the overflowing ashtray. But without fail, before we ever really got into it, something would remind us that it was almost time for *Jeopardy*. After some digging and scrambling, we'd find the

RANDY

remote control and change the channel just in time to watch Alex Trebek take his place behind the podium. Then one of us would spoon some more cocaine onto the little glass plate sitting at the center of the antique coffee table that somebody found in the alley. I'll take dramatic irony for $200, Alex.

I spent almost ten years sitting on the couch across from Randy. Sometimes we were joined by a few other interesting characters, each with their own complicated story. But more often than not, it was just the two of us. There were times when Randy and I would spend close to an entire day in his living room, snorting line after line and talking and talking and talking and talking. So, I got to know Randy pretty well. And I can tell you that Randy didn't tell those stories about his dad because he wanted to teach everyone how to be a parent. He talked about his dad because he loved him, and he missed him more than anyone knew. Randy's dad died about five years before I started spending time on the couch across from him, but the stories he told kept his dad alive and allowed Randy to tell anyone who would listen that his father was a good man who taught him so much before cancer ended his life too soon.

It was almost immediately clear to me that Randy's dad was his hero, his flawed and unmistakably human hero, much like my dad was to me. Unfortunately, part of what Randy's dad seemed to have passed on to him was the belief that expressing any emotion other than anger was a sign of weakness. It was this unbending belief that made it difficult for Randy to openly grieve the loss of his father, or even to suggest that he felt anything resembling sadness. On the other hand, I have been known to shed a tear or two during an especially moving episode of *The Golden Girls*. But when my hero-dad got sick and eventually died, I learned how deeply the illness and death of Randy's father affected him. I could finally see what Randy "was dealing with." And, from that point forward, there was a noticeable difference in the way he treated me, and in the way we talked to each other. I could tell that Randy understood the pain I felt, and that he desperately wanted to help.

Randy and I had a little tradition of locking ourselves in his apartment on Father's Day for a few years. We both loved watching golf with our dads when they were alive, so Randy and I would spend the entire day watching the final round of the U.S. Open on TV and telling stories about our fathers. We called it "No Dad Day," and I think we both kind of looked forward to it.

Unfortunately, despite all of Randy's good intentions, there wasn't anything he could've done that would've altered my course. My eventual self-destruction was completely out of his control, and my arrival at rock bottom was inevitable.

RANDY

I needed professional help and lots of it. Obviously, Randy wasn't properly equipped to provide the kind of healthy and appropriate support I needed during this personal crisis. But I will never forget how hard he tried to help me.

CHRIS
MY BROTHER

When I met my brother, Chris, outside of a friend's apartment, just a few hours after the news of my suspension from work and the impending criminal investigation broke, he hugged me. It was a real hug, not a see-you-soon-hug shared between brothers after Christmas Eve dinner. His empathy that day was palpable.

After the hug, Chris kept one hand on my shoulder and gave me a look that seemed to say, "This sucks, huh?" There wasn't even a hint of, "What the fuck is your problem?" That would've been much closer to the reaction I expected from him due to the pretty typical and outdated big brother–little brother dynamic Chris and I had been dealing with for as long as I can remember. Once I had finished soaking in that unfamiliar look on his face, Chris took a step back and told me to give him a dollar. I was noticeably confused by this request until he told me that the dollar would function as his retainer.

Chris is a lawyer, not the kind of lawyer I would eventually need to represent me in court, but a lawyer, nonetheless. More importantly, Chris is a very successful lawyer in the city where the charges against me would eventually be filed. I mention this not to draw any more attention to my big brother's success. Trust me on that. Chris's seemingly boundless success has always been kind of a sore spot for me. I mention it, instead, because it's relevant...and I guess I'm impressed by his success and a little proud of him, too, but let's just agree to never bring that up at Thanksgiving dinner or anywhere else, for that matter.

This is all relevant because Chris's work experience and connections would come in handy when the impending criminal charges against me became a reality. But Chris's status as a lawyer in Illinois also meant that he could be *my* lawyer, even for a modest retainer. I could tell him the

CHRIS

whole story under attorney-client privilege, and he wouldn't have to disclose anything I was about to unload onto him. I remember being embarrassed by the fact that I only had a few quarters in my pockets, but I did put them right into Chris's outstretched palm before I started talking. It's funny to think that, of all things, I was somehow ashamed about being broke that day.

I honestly don't remember if I was high that morning, or if I had slept much in the days leading up to it, or if I was coming down, drunk, paranoid, or anything else. I'm sure I wasn't alright, and it is safe to say that I wasn't sober either. I hadn't been truly sober for a stretch lasting longer than a day or two for almost three years at that point. I was either using cocaine, trying to find a way to use cocaine, or working on covering my tracks at all times. And it was exhausting.

When people imagine the life of a drug addict, they often envision us getting high and partying, and late nights with music, adventure, and fun. And although it's true that it was adventurous at times, the fun had ceased a long time ago. And the feeling I was getting from cocaine at that point could hardly be described as any kind of high. I hadn't had much fun using drugs for years, at least not since the day I flew down to

Oklahoma with my brother and learned that our dad had a brain tumor that would kill him in a matter of months.

After offering me a hug, Chris asked me to tell him the whole story. He said he needed to know all of the details to truly help me or find the people who would be best qualified to help me. It was a clear, fall day, probably around seventy degrees. Normally, this would be my favorite kind of day. And as my brother and I walked slowly through one of the oldest and nicest neighborhoods in the city, I just started to talk. I had been holding on to so many secrets for so long that I felt almost immediate relief as I began unloading the truth onto my brother that morning.

And I didn't even think about keeping any of the details to myself. I wanted so badly to get it all out. I wanted to come clean, stop the bleeding, and get help. There is a common saying in recovery that we are only as sick as our secrets. And I can't possibly express how true that was for me. I was extremely sick. I had been living a lie for so long and hiding the truth from everyone who cared about me. And it was torturous. It ate away at my conscience every day. That was the shame and guilt that served as fuel for my addiction until I found my back against the wall. Only then was I forced to pull back the curtain and reveal everything I had been working so hard to keep concealed.

CHRIS

I'm still surprised at how easily the truth flowed from my lips that day. Normally, telling anyone that you have been a closet drug addict for years, that you committed several sex crimes, cheated on your wife, most likely destroyed your family, and lost your dream job would be daunting. But to truly appreciate how unimaginably frightening this conversation could have been for me, you'd have to be familiar with the person I was telling, and you'd have to be aware of the complicated nature of what it was like to be his little brother. But the fact is, when it came down to it, I had no problem telling Chris my darkest secrets. And he responded with nothing but love and genuine empathy.

This all but proves that the innumerable insecurities and fears that I'd had about my relationship with Chris were petty, immature, and almost baseless...*almost*. That day, probably right after the hug, I realized I should have let it go years earlier. There is no doubt that it had been a challenge to grow up in the shadow cast by an overachiever of the highest order, and I don't want to minimize the impact of the way Chris bullied and belittled me when I was a kid. But that was forever ago, and he was a kid then too. The way he big-brothered me thirty years ago, and the way his seemingly limitless success has made it sometimes difficult for me to find my own identity or to feel competent and worthy, shouldn't have weighed on me so heavily for so long. And that morning outside of some coffee shop, I let go of almost all of that extra weight I'd been carrying with me since childhood, and that has made all the difference.

Chris did not just walk away and pat himself on the back after we were done talking that morning. After helping me unburden myself of all the dangerous secrets I'd been holding on to, he moved on to what I can only assume was a multi-step action plan that probably exists in some living document on his phone today. And Chris has continued to hold me up, encourage me, and support me ever since.

Some of what he has done is obvious. That day, when my full confession was complete, Chris took me to his house and booked a flight to Minnesota for us. And he stayed with me until he got me to rehab sometime the following afternoon. One of the counselors at the facility finally had to tell him to leave. But before his flight landed back in Chicago, Chris had already put together a team of lawyers that would make OJ blush. And, of course, Chris made sure they all knew where to send the bill. And he hasn't mentioned that to me once in the years since it all went down. But Chris didn't just do the research and write the checks. My brother was with me every step of the way. He checked in with my lawyers regularly, and he came with me to as many of my court dates

CHRIS

as he possibly could. If for some reason he couldn't be there, he always made sure to call me before and after to debrief and strategize. Again, this is just how Chris showed up for me while I was in the midst of the crisis of a lifetime.

But even after the dust settled and I didn't have to go to prison, I still needed plenty of help. I was certainly in no shape to be self-sufficient, and my new circumstances made living what I used to consider a normal and productive life pretty difficult. I'm not sure if Chris is aware that I know this, but he was also back-dooring some money to my mom for a while to help subsidize my housing and general livelihood. Obviously, part of this was Chris's effort to help my two sons, who shouldn't have to suffer for the mistakes their dad made, but I have no doubt that he would have done just as much to hold me up and support me, even if I was on my own.

And speaking of my two boys, a year or two after my conviction, Chris made the incredibly generous gesture of starting college funds for them. And on top of that, Chris gave me a "wink-wink" assurance that he would continue to contribute to those funds in the coming years, something he knew I would have a hard time doing now that my rich and fulfilling career had come to an abrupt end. And now that I found a way to get those winks published here, he'd look like a real jerk if he didn't follow through, right? See what I did there?

At the core, though, none of it is about money. Chris knows I don't really give a shit about that. It's about unconditional love and loyalty. It's about happiness and family. Chris's heart is as big as anyone's. I've suspected it my whole life, but I'm finally done collecting evidence to prove it. It's the truth.

If I've learned anything at all in the last six years, it's that all of us are constantly evolving and that everyone has character defects to deal with. And although I'm sure Chris would be hesitant to admit it, he is no exception to this rule. What separates people, though, is our willingness to address those defects and learn…so we can get better as we grow old. Our own father, the man who raised me and Chris with remarkably different results, was a perfect example of this kind of growth. And both Chris and I are immeasurably better men than we were twenty years ago. Nobody who knows us would dare argue against that fact. I have no doubt that our dad would be proud of both of us for not settling into some easy, asshole personality. And I'm sure Chris and I will be forever grateful for the way our dad modeled manhood for the two of us while he was still alive.

WAYNE
A DRUG ADDICT

When I was in junior high, I spent a few weeks each summer at a camp in the Minnesota Northwoods. It was everything a kid like me could dream of: canoeing, kayaking, swimming, archery, riflery, campfires, and sing-alongs. I just ate it up. I'm realizing now that the inpatient rehab facility I went to was only a few lakes over from that old camp, and some of my days in rehab were oddly similar to my junior high camp experience—although, the rehab facility rarely let us shoot guns and locked up the canoes at night so we wouldn't be tempted to use them to paddle our way over to the bar on the other side of the lake. Regardless, my thirty-seven days of inpatient rehab felt a lot like camp to me. And Wayne was just like so many of the camp friends I made thirty years earlier.

Wayne introduced himself to me when he picked me up from the medical unit. This is where all patients spent at least a night or two before transitioning into the general population "houses" located in a different building. Although the facility I found myself in was indeed in Minnesota, its patients came from all around the world. Wayne was from North Dakota, but I instantly recognized him as "Minnesota nice."

There had to be a geographic link to this particular personality quirk. I come from a long line of proud Minnesotans; therefore, I am a skilled locator of other residents and descendants of the land of more than ten thousand lakes. If you've ever met an authentic Minnesotan, then you are already familiar with some of their most pronounced character traits. And at the top of that list is a type of genuine kindness and warmth that has an almost supernatural capability of making you feel instantly calm and comfortable. I'm just now realizing how this makes Minnesota the perfect location for any person amid a crisis. Needless to say, Wayne's presence and

WAYNE

natural demeanor as he came in for one of those handshake man-hugs left me feeling instantly relaxed and right at home. Over the next month or so, I would get to know Wayne very well, and although we haven't stayed in contact with each other over the years, we bonded like brothers during a critical moment in both of our lives.

After spending a day or two getting used to the structure and feel of our daily treatment schedule, I was all in. I had by no means forgotten about the mess I left behind when I took off for rehab, but I was finally getting clean and could feel the tangled web in my mind finally beginning to clear up. The very early stage of recovery when you start to feel better than you have in a long time is often referred to as the "pink cloud." It's during this stage that your mind and body are beginning to heal themselves as the final remnants of your addiction slowly clear out of your system. It's easy to get lost in the positive glow of the pink cloud, but in the end, it's just a cloud and will not hold you up forever. The problems you created will be there waiting for you when the pink cloud inevitably dissipates in the winds of reality. But I rode that pink cloud as far as I could, and I dove headfirst into the whole treatment process.

Wayne was riding shotgun on the same pink cloud after one of our group therapy sessions when we decided to take a walk around the lake during our free time. This is when I learned more of the specifics of Wayne's story. We had our version of the "what are you in for?" conversation that you may be familiar with if you've ever seen a movie set in a jail or a prison. Coincidentally, both Wayne and I were facing potential legal problems on the home front. He was more willing and able to discuss the details of his alleged crimes, and that was hard for me at first. My brother/lawyer had instructed me not to talk to anyone about my illegal activities or the ongoing investigation that was taking place. But I found it extremely difficult to dance around the subject altogether because it was obviously significant. But for the majority of my stay in Minnesota, I saved those conversations for the individual therapy sessions with my counselor.

Wayne, on the other hand, came clean to me on our first walk. Right up until the day he left for treatment, he was on the wrong end of several visits from detectives who were investigating multiple thefts of copper wire in the area where Wayne lived and worked. Well, turns out, Wayne was just as guilty as I was. And, although his crimes seemed far less serious than mine in every way imaginable, it was still possible that he would be charged with several felonies as a result of a seemingly victimless crime spree Wayne embarked on as a means to fund his increasingly problematic addiction to opiates.

WAYNE

Wayne was a union lineman. Not one of those big fellas that protect the quarterback, but a professional tradesman who constructed and maintained electric power lines. An interesting job that I'm sure my dad would've had a lot more questions about. It was a job-related injury that led to Wayne's introduction to opiates. He underwent a serious but successful surgery to address some damage done to his neck and back during an incident at work. The initial injury and the rehabilitation and recovery from the surgery left Wayne in constant and almost unbearable pain. He found himself popping his prescribed painkillers by the handful. And what the doctor was prescribing him never seemed like enough.

Eventually, Wayne felt like he needed to find another source for the pills he believed he needed to get back to work and avoid losing his job altogether. Making the situation even more desperate was the fact that Wayne had a two-year-old baby at home and another one on the way. Wayne didn't have any connections to the drug-dealing world, but it turns out he did know someone who had a refillable prescription for methadone. It seemed like his only option at the time, so he offered to buy her methadone for a price that could make her life a little easier too. Well, eventually, that wasn't enough either. This increasing tolerance that is especially common with opiate users is what usually signals trouble on the horizon.

Like many drug addicts who aren't in recovery, Wayne found himself in some pretty significant financial trouble. And with a baby on the way, the timing couldn't have been worse. This is when Wayne came up with the plan that could have landed him in prison. Whenever his crew was finished with a job, they were instructed to leave any leftover copper in the dumpsters on the job site. The customers paid for it whether they used it or not, so they were told to leave it. Wayne decided there wasn't much harm or risk if he just put some of that copper in the back of his truck. He could then take it to a scrap yard and walk away with some of the cash he so desperately needed. And this is exactly what he did for almost a year to afford the increasing cost of his drug habit. The problem was, he had to take more and more copper as his tolerance to methadone continued to increase. Eventually, it was too much to go unnoticed, and the authorities caught on. I think he ended up cutting some sort of plea deal that allowed him to avoid prison (I really hope so, anyway), but I'm guessing he was no longer allowed to be a member of the lineman's union. And Wayne didn't have a plan B.

Our pending legal issues aside, Wayne and I had a lot to talk about on what turned out to be our sometimes twice-daily walks around the lake. And we managed to make each

WAYNE

other laugh, even in the midst of the shitstorms we created for ourselves. I won't forget when his pregnant wife and his daughter came to see him on one of the family visitation days. I could tell what a great father and husband Wayne was. And it meant a lot that he invited me to have dinner with him and his family that night.

But one thing kept eating away at my conscience, and the closer we got to our discharge dates, it only got worse. I felt like I needed to tell Wayne what I did. I didn't like having new secrets already. It was a familiar feeling that had only caused trouble for me in the past. I needed to get it off my chest for my own sake, but I also felt like I owed it to him as a friend and brother whom I'd grown so close to. And it was one of the last things I did before I checked out.

Wayne and I went for one last walk around the lake, and I just let my story spill out. I tried to explain why I didn't tell him the whole truth sooner, but he didn't seem to need that. Wayne gave me another half-handshake man-hug and told me that he would never judge me. He said it was clear to him what kind of man I was, and whatever I did or didn't do with one of my former students couldn't change that. That was the first of many times I received reactions like that when I would eventually gain the courage to tell my story to other addicts and alcoholics. If there is a group of people who are going to let some shit slide, to look past a few mistakes and see a person for who they really are, it's us. In fact, I'd say that's one of the best things about us.

DAVID
A DRUG ADDICT

The rehab facility I checked into was the one I always knew I would check into. Not only was it in the woods in Minnesota, a place full of nostalgic comfort for me, it was also one of the very best rehab facilities in the country. I'd known about it for a long time, in part because I was not the first person in my family to show up at their doors looking for help, but also because it was the place where celebrities were sometimes known to go to jump-start their recovery. And a few of those big names happened to belong to people

I admired at some point in my life. I don't like admitting this, but part of me was excited to go to rehab because I thought I might end up spending a month in group therapy with some big-name celebrity.

About a week into my treatment, I managed to take over Wayne's old job, and I got the assignment to go down to the medical unit to greet and escort the newest member of my rehab group back to our "house." He was pleasant and a little scared but happy to be out of the medical unit, as all of us were when we first arrived. It wasn't until a few days later that I learned of my new house member's bona fide celebrity status. None of us had ever heard of him or anything he had done to become famous, but he was a celebrity nonetheless.

David's appearance drew the attention of every patient and staff member immediately. He wore sweatpants and an old t-shirt like the rest of us, but every head turned to gawk at him in every room he entered. But none of us knew anything about him. It finally started to make sense when David confided in me and told me that, in his country, he was maybe the biggest star on TV. It isn't uncommon for any of us to exaggerate or tell half-true, big stories about our lives during treatment, so I wasn't too quick to accept this news about David's life outside of our Northwoods retreat. But I think he sensed my skepticism and decided on an easy way to settle any of my concerns.

DAVID

He took me over to one of the computers we were allowed to use to check email, look for jobs, and check football scores. David told me he needed my help with his Twitter account because the press in his country reported that he had died of an overdose. This much was true. We sat there and read one of the articles together. He knew I was an English teacher, and he wanted my help writing a tweet that would appropriately and respectfully announce that he was still breathing. Once we settled on a simple, concise, but vague statement to post, we did some surface-level googling that unearthed the true nature and reach of his fame...as if his millions of Twitter followers wasn't evidence enough.

Without divulging too much, I'll just say that, in many ways, he is on the same level of fame as Heath Ledger, Amy Winehouse, or Ben Affleck. But in Minnesota that fall, he was also on the same level as the rest of the addicts and alcoholics trying to get healthy again. I could tell that David needed this escape from the spotlight he was used to, and I got the feeling he didn't want to go back. Over time, he told me his story, and it was powerful and full of lessons I will never forget. David and I lost touch a few years ago, but I have to admit that I still google him more than a few times a year, just to make sure he's still alive.

BRADLEY
AN ALCOHOLIC

At the end of each day during my stay in the inpatient rehab facility, I gathered with the other men in my unit for a group meeting and meditation. The meeting had a very specific format and structure that was meant to help us internalize some healthy and practical behaviors in hopes that some of these behaviors would translate into our lives on the outside. Two of my housemates would lead the meeting, guiding us through a few readings from the twelve-step literature and a discussion of our daily chores in the house. Once we got through that, one person was tasked with reading the weather forecast, someone else gave us a couple of headlines from the news, and another person told a joke.

But my favorite part of the meeting, by a longshot, was the reading of the promises. This is how we concluded each and every meeting we had. The promises can be found in the big book (this is what we call the Alcoholics Anonymous textbook). This particular passage, from a chapter called "Into Action," outlines what *should* happen if addicts and alcoholics follow the twelve steps and then continue to live them in recovery. It's the most dog-eared section of every addict's big book. Ask any alcoholic or addict in recovery where to find the promises. Most of them will be able to give you the page number without thinking twice.

We appreciate hearing these promises early in recovery, and we find ourselves going back to them over and over as we move forward, sometimes without seeing any obvious results. The truth is, our lives often continue to get worse for a while when we give up drinking and drugging. The problems we created and the messes we made as we nosedived into the bowels of our addiction were still there when we sobered up. And that can be really hard to swallow.

BRADLEY

It was most definitely an early roadblock for me. I went to rehab for the first time just as my real problems were beginning to show their faces. And once I finally got sober, I could really feel the impact of what I had done. It sucked. And to be honest, for months, if not years, all I wanted to do was get high and run from the guilt and shame I was feeling.

During most of my inpatient treatment, Bradley from Baltimore was in charge of reading the promises. Bradley was in his thirties. He was muscular and covered in tattoos, but he was kindhearted and a little shy. He was basically single-handedly raising a child of one of his ex-girlfriends, and he also had PTSD, a parting gift for his two tours as a frontline soldier in Iraq. Bradley's story was like many others I've heard over the years. He came back from Iraq, and he couldn't shake the images, sounds, and smells of war. He couldn't just go about his life like he didn't witness and experience the horrors of the battlefield. And on top of that, Bradley didn't feel supported by anyone in his community. And if anyone did dare to reach out to him, he found it hard to take them seriously because he knew there was no way anyone could possibly understand what he had been through. I remember Bradley telling me that war is one of those things that you can't understand by reading books or listening to the stories brought home by veterans. He often reminded me that war is one of only a few "you have to be there" experiences. And Bradley despised when people used war metaphors when talking about sports.

The trauma of war and Bradley's unstable relationships at home led him almost directly to the bottle. At first, it was just in the garage at night while he worked on his car, but eventually, he found himself drinking in the garage from morning until night. And the more he drank, the angrier he got, the more he felt cheated by life, and the more serious his PTSD symptoms became. After several months of this, Bradley found his breaking point. I don't recall all of the details, but it ended with him being arrested and charged with assault after an altercation with a neighbor. The child he was raising, the only positive light in Bradley's life at that time, ended up going back to live with her abusive mother hundreds of miles away. A few weeks later, Bradley finally hit rock bottom, and somehow he got himself to Minnesota and into treatment. To this day, he is one of the only people I've met in recovery who got themselves through the doors of a treatment center without any pushing, prodding, or support from anyone else.

The reading of the promises is something that happened in all of the units of my rehab facility each and every night, but I'm sure none of the other readers carried out their duty with the same fervor that Bradley brought to his job. First of all, Bradley stood on the table in the middle of the room. And he didn't need the big book to remember the promises. He just jumped up onto the table and ordered all of the "drunks and junkies" to stand up and gather around him. Then he started yelling like a substitute teacher. Eventually, all thirty of us would be participating in what felt to me like some kind of shouted prayer. Bradley always added a few F-bombs to give the promises a little more pop (I remember thinking that it made him sound like a drill sergeant from the movies). But other than that, Bradley stuck to the script. And after listing the many positive outcomes that we were sure to receive if we were painstaking about this phase of our development, Bradley repeated the final question from the end of the promises section of the big book three or four times: "Are these extravagant promises? Are these extravagant promises? Are these extravagant promises?" And by this time, Bradley was stomping on the table (I'm imagining him wearing combat boots now, but it probably just seemed that way) and using both of his hands to point to the members of his platoon. Each time he asked us, we responded the same way: "We think not!"

When Bradley was satisfied, he would jump down from the table, and we'd all exchange man-hugs for a few minutes. Then we'd make our way to our beds and put our heads on our pillows, believing that recovery was possible and that our lives were bound to get better.

I haven't heard from Bradley for a few years now, but I sure hope that he's winning his battle against addiction and that the promises are coming true in his daily life. Also, I hope he doesn't mind that I just used a war metaphor to talk about his addiction. But I have a feeling he'll understand.

AN EIGHTEEN-YEAR-OLD BOY IN A COOK COUNTY JAIL CELL

After turning myself in and spending one long, cold, and lonely night in a small cell inside the first precinct police station, the dented and damaged metal door I'd been staring at for hours swung open without any notice at all. Using an odd assortment of grunts and aggressive body language, the officer herded me into a narrow hallway with several other inmates. Another officer then took over and shouted instructions at us for several minutes. A few of the inmates had questions or concerns about the process and order of events for the day. The officer just repeated the instructions word for word, a little bit louder each time, effectively ending the question-and-answer portion of his presentation.

All of us were to be transferred by police van to Cook County Jail at the corner of 26th and California. I was scared beyond belief. Frozen and speechless. I was handcuffed and chained to a young Latino man who was quite vociferously expressing his anger about an alleged beating he received from the Chicago police officer who arrested him the night before. This did not please the officers tasked with cuffing us and loading the vans. And I was beginning to worry that I might catch some of the next beating this young man would get at the hands of the Chicago Police. But after narrowly avoiding any additional physical conflict with the officers, we were "safely" locked into the back of the old police van. It was only then that I got the chance to look closer at the man I was connected to at the wrist and ankle.

His face was cut and badly bruised. He had a dirty bandage wrapped haphazardly around his left wrist, and he was having some difficulty walking. His pain was real and obvious. And my Spanish was just good enough to understand that he was

AN EIGHTEEN-YEAR-OLD BOY

not thrilled about being handcuffed and chained to me, of all people. On the other hand, the rest of the inmates sharing the metal benches with us in the back of the police van found it hilarious. One thing was clear: I wasn't alone any longer. But I was already missing the cold and dark cell I had just spent the night in. I knew this was going to happen, but I think there was a part of me that had been holding on to some false hope that my fears were baseless and founded on flimsy generalizations. But the truth is, all of the wit, wisdom, and charm I inherited from my dad wasn't going to help me blend in or get through that day, not to mention any future days I could spend in jail or prison. And the prison time I was potentially facing wouldn't be counted in days. The deep dread of that possible fate weighed on me for almost three more years.

Although I was initially placed in protective custody (what a few of the officers called "the players club") due to the nature of my charges and the public attention my case was sure to receive, I was routinely shuffled, shoved, dragged, or pulled into cells with several other inmates in the bowels of the Cook County Jail. And it wasn't long before they all knew what I was in for. My lawyer told me countless times as I prepared for this day that I should just keep my head down and say I got "caught up in some shit" if anyone were to ask me what I was in for. And he assured me that they would be asking. That plan went out the window almost immediately, though. The thing is, they have TVs in Cook County Jail, lots of them. And I was all over the news that morning…plus my mug shot, my name, the numerous sexual assault charges I was facing, the pictures and live shots of the school where I worked and once attended as a student, the school where my wife was teaching history, even on that day, as the reporters gathered outside.

    I joined three other inmates in a small cell as I waited to be called for my bond hearing. I was only feet from the courtroom, from the judge, from my brother, and from the press, but I couldn't process any of it. It felt like I was under some sort of spell. I remember thinking that it kind of seemed like I'd taken too much cough syrup or something. And sitting directly across from me in that holding cell was a boy, maybe eighteen years old. He was wearing a paper jumpsuit that the detectives gave to him the night before when they took his clothes as part of their investigation. He was charged with murder, but his case didn't make the news that morning. It wasn't considered news in Chicago. Cases like his are relatively commonplace, and sadly, the general public rarely shows any interest in learning the truth about them or finding the root causes of crimes like the one he was charged with. I don't think they would like what they would find if they took the time to look a little closer.

AN EIGHTEEN-YEAR-OLD BOY

The two of us sat in that small cell for almost two hours, along with a man who was arrested at the airport the night before. I spent most of that time thinking about how much this teenaged boy reminded me of so many of the students I'd taught over the years. And his face made it clear that he was just as scared as I was. Like me, this kid had no idea what was coming. But that's where the similarities ended.

Violent crime statistics suggest that the eighteen-year-old across from me in that cell probably grew up in a community with underfunded schools and limited resources or opportunities for positive after-school programs. He most likely received inadequate healthcare and did not have easy access to any needed social services. The odds are great that he lived his entire life surrounded by ubiquitous violence, drug use, and crime. And after facing all of those unnecessary obstacles, he was now facing the possibility of spending the rest of his life in prison and was represented by an overworked, underpaid public defender. And my cellmate was Black.

On the other hand, my team of lawyers represented the Daleys (yeah, those Daleys), and I am White. And I grew up in the suburbs, only a few blocks from one of the most dangerous neighborhoods in Chicago. The kid who was hugging his knees on the bench across from me that day might have lived just a few streets away. But on my side of the arbitrary boundary separating Chicago from the suburbs, the lawns were green and manicured, the schools were funded, the park district had a catalog full of after-school programs, violence was rare, the streetlights always worked, the police rarely harassed a resident, and people felt safe. I was well-nourished and afforded the best healthcare available. School social workers and psychologists were always available if I should ever need their services. And I was guilty of most of the charges against me. His guilt or innocence, whatever the court decided, is still a mystery in my eyes.

This is the hard truth: I didn't deserve to live my life on the side of the street with all of the resources, and the boy sitting across from me in that cell at 26th and California didn't deserve to live on the other side of the street. It was geographic luck. Period.

GLENN
A FRIEND

I spent approximately forty-four hours in Cook County Jail before my brother's connections and $15,000 in cash got me released on bond. My notably short incarceration left me traumatized, anxious, depressed, and generally pessimistic about my future, not to mention the future of my family. It was close to midnight when I passed through the appropriately imposing gates on 26th Street. I was handcuffed and exhausted in the backseat of a car driven by a Cook County

Sheriff's deputy, and I was without any measurable sense of hope. I will never forget that feeling. I need to carry the memory of that feeling with me forever. It's as important as any other memory I have.

For the next several months, I was on house arrest, living with my sister and her pregnant roommate, sleeping on an air mattress in their living room. It would be a full year before I would learn the legal consequences of what I had done. Twenty-two felonies were hanging in the balance. The best-case scenario was frightening and nearly impossible for me to grasp. The worst-case scenario, which I spent the most time imagining, was devastating and unspeakable. It was, in fact, the embodiment of every last one of my deepest, darkest, and worst fears.

The Cook County Sheriff's department gave me permission to leave the apartment to attend my outpatient rehab program for a few hours, four days a week, and to see my therapist once a week, as well. But that was it. The only opportunity I had to see my kids was for an hour or two on Sundays. My wife would make the long trip to the far north side of the city to drop them off at my sister's apartment. Then, during her only "time off" all week, she would run some errands, go to yoga, or do anything else that might give her even the briefest relief from the sadness and chaos she was living in. To say the least, this situation was far from ideal, but every time I looked in the mirror, I reminded myself that the broken man looking back at me was wholly responsible for making it happen. Eventually, I learned to stop hating myself for making the decisions I made, but I will never allow myself to forget that it was indeed me who made those decisions. Taking responsibility, holding myself accountable, and accepting the reality of what I did are absolutely essential if I truly intend to recover and make meaningful amends to those I've hurt. How else can I expect to learn, grow, and evolve?

On one of the darkest days of this torturous, doomsday-holding-pattern stage of my journey, my friend Glenn came by my sister's apartment to check on me, to keep me company, and maybe to get some more of the story. It wasn't the first time I noticed how he often seemed to show up when I needed him the most. This is the kind of friend Glenn is. I knew he would be there. I knew he would somehow find a way to make me laugh. I knew he wouldn't even dream of judging me. And, more than anything else, I knew that he would offer me his unconditional support.

Glenn is one of those rare friends who truly means it when they say they would do anything for you. I can't count how many times he's offered to throw himself under the bus for me over the years. And now that the bus had run me over, and it was clear that it was going to back up and do it again and again over the next few years, Glenn seemed intent on helping me see that, contrary to how I was feeling at the moment, things weren't all that bad. In fact, Glenn was prepared to convince me that this terrible mess that I made for myself and my loved ones may actually be a positive thing, something I would one day be grateful for. There was no way I could accurately express to him how impossible and ridiculous that seemed to me at the time, but I tried desperately to let him know that he was wasting his energy if he was attempting to expose to me even the faintest silver-lining to the nightmare I was living. At times, I actually despised him for refusing to just listen to me and acknowledge the undeniable fact that several lives, including my own, were completely ruined as a result of my selfish, irresponsible, and despicable behavior.

When I eventually confessed to Glenn that I had given up any of the remaining hope that I had been clinging to, when I told him that I was sure that I was headed to prison and that I had most likely caused irreparable emotional damage to my family members and countless others, that my life was, in effect, finished, he just told me to stop believing that. He said it so matter-of-factly that, for a second, I almost thought it could be possible. Glenn and I have continued that conversation for years now, and after careful consideration, and

GLENN

what can only be described as stubbornly skeptical reflection, I am willing to admit (only Glenn knows how hard this is for me) that maybe he was at least a little bit right. Maybe I did have some power over what I did or didn't believe, and maybe those beliefs were, in some way, vaguely connected to how my life would eventually unfold. Maybe.

DAISY
AN ALCOHOLIC

The night I met Daisy, she spent hours on the living room floor of the apartment she shared with a close friend of mine from my most recent stint in an intensive outpatient rehab program. She was propped up against the wall, sweating, trembling, and puking into a plastic grocery bag, but she managed to get some deodorant on and squeeze into her jeans in time to get to her part-time job at Nordstrom Rack by 1:00 p.m. the next day. That was the first time I ever witnessed the truly awful reality of alcohol withdrawal.

Daisy's roommate was an ICU nurse, and she knew exactly how to manage this sometimes-deadly situation. So the three of us stayed up all night making sure Daisy didn't die. I'll never forget how anxious, scared, and sad I was as I tried to make jokes and distract her from the pain she was feeling or how lucky I felt that it wasn't me. It's a part of the disease that I will never have to endure personally, but it wasn't the last time I'd spend the night making sure Daisy wouldn't pass out in the bathtub, fall down, or choke to death on her own vomit.

Daisy used to be a speech pathologist in an assisted living home for senior citizens. She was making a difference and feeling almost normal. That's what she got her degree for, and that's the job she wished she was on her way to the afternoon after I met her, as she tried to hide her dry heaves on the Chicago Avenue bus. But, in the midst of her downward spiral into alcoholism about a year before I met her, Daisy got drunk and crashed her first car into a few small trees on the way to the job she worked so hard to get. She remembers flirting with the cops who arrested her that day. She checked into rehab shortly thereafter, and now she uses her master's degree to work retail on Michigan Avenue. She jokes about it, but I can tell it bothers her.

Daisy's mom, who used to have a husband like this, is so tired. She's been through enough to know that her daughter will live or die, be happy or miserable... and that there is almost nothing she can do to get in the way of it. But that doesn't make it any easier for her to let go. She raised Daisy alone, and until Daisy's disease had a firm grip on her life, they had a positive, loving, and meaningful relationship. Daisy considered her mom her best friend. I'm sure her mom feels responsible for the sadness and pain her daughter feels today. I'm sure she would do anything to make her baby happy and healthy again. Daisy's suffering probably weighs on her mom every day, and the profound sadness and guilt she feels is likely debilitating.

And I imagine Daisy loathes the way her disease affects her mother. I wouldn't be surprised if it was the first thing she thinks about when she wakes up each morning and wishes she could do something to reverse it. But alcoholism and addiction don't work like that. Daisy can't just close her eyes and pray, or meditate, or write in her journal, or think positive thoughts and make it stop hurting people. In fact, when an alcoholic tries to do just that, and it doesn't work, it only provides fuel for their relentless instinct to drink. Daisy is not weak; she is sick. This is what so many people don't understand about addiction. And it is exactly why people like us can't just get better by trying harder and why it infuriates us when people dare to imply that we can. All of us try really fucking hard, but our seemingly inevitable failure can be devastating.

"I've never had a bad day in my whole life." This is how Daisy's dad responds every time she asks him how he's doing. It's a sad and obvious lie, but Daisy still smiles when she hears her dad's response. And she calls him almost every day. But when they are done swapping stories over the phone, Daisy doesn't censor her feelings about what kind of dad he has been. No doubt Daisy is well aware of the hypocrisy and irony in his late-night words of wisdom. But he's right. And maybe his advice carries more weight with her than anything else. It's something we all realize, I think. That we can't really take anyone seriously unless they've been there, like really been there. And Daisy's dad has been there. In fact, he's still there, fighting just as hard as she is. He's been at it for years. And that means a lot to Daisy.

"Daisy, someday in your life, you're going to want to go places. You need to stand outside of the circle and look at yourself."

"I know, Dad. You're right."

Daisy's dad tells her to go for walks. To take care of her business *before* she drinks. To grab life by the neck like a tiger. And he doesn't place judgment on her. And he always answers the phone. And he always tells her that he loves her before they hang up.

Daisy sees how her dad's disease has impacted his relationships with his family. And she listens with compassion as her

DAISY

aunt explains how hard it has been for her to let him go, how sad she is for their mom, especially.

Daisy has told me that she desperately wants to help her dad, but she is worried that it's too late for him. She has also said that she's frightened she will end up as sick, sad, alone, and full of regret as he seems to be. But I hope she realizes that it is not too late for her. I know she can't do it alone, nobody can, but I know Daisy has all the courage, strength, and heart necessary to find her true self again, to live the life she has always wanted. All she needs to do is ask for help and accept it without reservation. Unfortunately, this may be the hardest thing for any addict or alcoholic to do.

KYLE
A DRUG ADDICT

Kyle is tall and handsome, and young. He had just turned twenty-two when I met him, and he appeared to be relatively happy and healthy. At first glance, despite his unrelenting pursuit of the record for most days without changing his dirty sweatpants award, he looked more like he should be on some MTV spring break special instead of sitting in the chair next to me in a group therapy session at an outpatient drug rehab facility in Chicago. Kyle's disease, like most of ours, was mostly invisible to the naked eye. But there is no doubt that it was killing him. If addiction was classified in the same manner as cancer, Kyles's addiction was stage four at the very least when I met him. His condition was critical, and his chances for a full recovery were bleak. This was Kyle's third stint in rehab, and it was clear that the past unsuccessful attempts to treat his disease had done significant damage to whatever hope he had of returning to college and eventually living the normal and healthy life he deserved.

Kyle was one of the patients in my group who was also living in the residential facility attached to the treatment center. This meant that, if he so desired, he could avoid going outside for days at a time. And although the counselors and other staff discouraged such behavior, Kyle managed to spend entire days in his pajamas and slippers. But something about Kyle made me think that his demeanor in treatment was some sort of defense mechanism and that, underneath that apathetic front he put up every day, there was a really good kid who desperately wanted to get better. In more than one way, Kyle reminded me of the way I was when I was about his age. I hated myself back then, and I had a feeling that Kyle didn't feel great about himself either. Eventually, I decided that, for better or worse, I would have a little sit down with Kyle and let him know how I felt about the way he was approaching his treatment and recovery.

KYLE

Over the course of my multiple stints in treatment, it was not uncommon for me to find a case like Kyle and decide to take it upon myself to step in and save the day. Looking back, I believe that I did help most of these people in one way or another, but at what cost? My persistent inability to maintain healthy boundaries hasn't been an easy one to get under control. It is clear that I didn't leave my instinct to teach and mentor young people on the front lawn of the high school the day I was asked to leave, knowing in my heart that I was most likely never to return. But how much of my instinct to help others is related to my inability to help myself? What part of my behavior was selfless and virtuous, and what part was rooted in a selfish desire to soothe my aching conscience?

In one form or another, I have always hated something about myself. At times, I hated *everything* about myself, but I finally had something to feel good about when I was teaching and making a difference. It was a source of great pride in my life, and although it's a bit muddied now, I will continue to be proud of the work I did as a teacher, coach, and club sponsor. I cannot possibly quantify how rewarding it was when I knew that, even in the slightest way, my efforts made some kind of positive impact on the life of even one of my students. The seemingly sad truth is that, at every turn, my good deeds probably benefited me more than any of the students I was trying to help. I think it's what Nietzsche calls "virtuous selfishness." But I still struggle with the feeling that, for me, it was more selfish than virtuous.

My efforts to help Kyle fizzled out over time, and I would consider the mission to be one of my most disappointing failures to date. Although we have stayed in contact on and off over the years, it seems that things are only getting worse each time I see him. He's one of the few people I have developed a close and meaningful relationship with since my journey began, and I can't shake the feeling that I'm going to get one of those awful phone calls one day informing me that the disease has taken another young person who would've lived a long and rewarding life otherwise.

Kyle grew up in one of the wealthiest suburbs of Chicago, and by all accounts, he had a childhood devoid of any major trauma. And he got along well with his parents. He was a talented basketball player and a gifted student with a witty sense of humor. His addiction has more inconspicuous roots than one comes to expect to hear about in rehab. It started for Kyle in much the same way it started for me. Kyle always liked to party, and he was a popular kid. Like me, he just never wanted the party to end. Kyle and I aren't the first kids to have that problem, but when you combine it with a predisposition for

KYLE

addiction or alcoholism, a disastrous downward spiral can be just one bad weekend away.

When Kyle finished high school, he headed to college in maybe the worst/best city for someone who never wants the party to end: New Orleans. Needless to say, Kyle didn't last long there. I went on an annual pilgrimage to New Orleans every summer when I was in college, and even though we only spent a few nights on Bourbon Street each year, it was a miracle I managed to get back home relatively unscathed. When Kyle arrived in the Big Easy, his vices predictably found friends and gathered steam. It wasn't long before Kyle became a low-level dealer, then a mid-level dealer, then a dealer on a level he didn't have any business being on. Eventually, there was some counterfeit money situation, the details of which aren't clear, but the Secret Service did show up at his parents' home, much to their surprise. Kyle's legal troubles were mounting when he finally overdosed on fentanyl nasal spray—something I hadn't even heard of until I met Kyle, and I had run in some pretty shady circles for a while.

Kyle has collected a few impressive stretches of sober time since we first met about five years ago, and he was enrolled for a time at one of Chicago's many quality universities. But it seems like his barrel has more than one false bottom. The last time I saw Kyle was pretty scary. He called another friend of ours and asked her to send an Uber for him and a friend to a neighborhood in Chicago that was a far cry from the one where he grew up. And after several calls and lots of debate, we convinced him to come to us. And we spent the night attempting to talk him out of what I can only describe as severely paranoid delusions.

When Kyle woke up the next afternoon, we made arrangements to get him somewhere safe, and we resisted all of his increasingly ridiculous requests for money. But I made a decision that day that I would steer clear of Kyle until I could be sure that he was healthy again. As much as I love that kid, I know that it wouldn't take much for him to pull me down to a dark place. It's a boundary I needed to set, and who knows how strong it is, but I feel good about how I've handled it so far. It's not his fault. He's sick. It's just plain sad. I'll never stop thinking the worst whenever I get a late-night call from some unknown number.

JAKE AND HENRY
A DRUG ADDICT AND HIS LITTLE BROTHER

Jake died the day before his twentieth birthday. His mom found his cold and lifeless body sitting slouched against his bed that morning. It appeared that he died with his head in his hands. There was a recently used needle at his side, next to a small baggie that once contained what Jake thought was run-of-the-mill heroin. Turns out, that small bag that he bought a couple of blocks east of Austin Boulevard the night before was laced with fentanyl, an opiate one hundred times the strength of morphine.

Fentanyl is sometimes used to cut the heroin from Mexico because the Mexican cartels can buy it cheap from China and add it to their product to increase the weight, value, and most importantly, their profit. It is a business decision that makes perfect sense, but sadly, this monetary gain comes with a loss of human life on both sides of the border. Heroin addicts have become well aware of the risk since the emergence of this fentanyl phenomenon, but the increased chance of sudden death does almost nothing to weaken the opiate addict's machine-like drive to get their fix. Like so many overdose deaths these days, Jake didn't die from taking too much heroin; he died from taking too much of a drug that he didn't even know he was putting into his body.

I met Jake in an outpatient treatment program in Chicago, but I learned about him from his little brother a couple of years earlier. Jake's brother, Henry, didn't talk much when he was a student in my American Literature class during his junior year. And to be honest, he didn't do much work either. But Henry almost always responded to the journal prompts that I put on the board to start each class period. For ten or fifteen minutes each day, Henry wrote about his brother, his brother's addiction, and how that addiction was affecting him and his family on a daily basis. Henry never volunteered to share what he wrote with the class, but he almost always let me read it. I remember one journal entry about how hard it was to share a room with Jake. Henry was almost constantly worried that Jake was dying. He would get up several times a night just to check if his big brother was still breathing. It was abundantly clear that Henry loved his older brother and that watching him succumb to this insidious disease was getting harder and harder for him to do.

After spending a year as Henry's teacher, I had a feeling that he was on a path similar to his brother's. On most days, I could tell that Henry was using drugs before, during, or after school. He was becoming more and more lethargic and apathetic, almost zombie-like on some days. I believed that Henry was enrolled in classes two academic tracks below where he belonged. And it is my assumption now that, over the years, Henry's growing disinterest in school was misinterpreted as a lack of intellectual and academic skills. I wonder what Henry's educational experience would've looked like if his older brother was never introduced to opiates.

The image most people conjure when they picture a heroin addict is nothing like Jake, but heroin addicts like Jake are the norm, not the exception. Jake was born and raised in a wealthy suburb just west of Chicago. He had two loving parents and all of the resources and support anyone could need. But Jake's undeniable privilege could not prevent his addiction from taking his life. In fact, it took less than four years for opiates to take Jake down. It all started with a football injury when he was sixteen. Just as it was becoming clear that Jake was a talented football player with a chance to play in college, he broke all the fingers in his right hand. After a complicated surgery, doctors prescribed the necessary medication to help Jake deal with the pain during his recovery. Jake's football career was over, and the countdown to his death began.

Before his injury, Jake occasionally drank, like many teenagers do, and smoked weed on a semi-regular basis, but that was the extent of his drinking and drug use. There weren't any obvious signs of Jake being on the road to addiction, overdose, and death. The opiates prescribed by the doctors helped Jake manage the pain in his hand and probably helped him deal with the mental and emotional pain stemming from his forced retirement from football. In fact, Jake sometimes bore the pain in his hand for most of the day so that he could take a triple dose of painkillers at night. He found this was the best way to silent his thoughts and distract him enough to get a good night's sleep. Jake got used to taking the pills for things other than the physical pain he felt, but eventually, the doctors would stop prescribing them. His hand was healed, but now he was hooked.

At this point, Jake had a choice. He was only seventeen, and he was facing a decision that would almost certainly determine his fate. Jake could start buying pills at school or on the street, or he could suffer terrible opiate withdrawals and be incredibly sick for a few days. Potentially, Jake could die if he tried to withdraw without medical attention. If he had chosen this option, there is no guarantee that he would have avoided death the day before his twentieth birthday, but it certainly would have increased his chances of living the long and happy life that he deserved.

The pills that Jake started buying to keep his head calm and to prevent the withdrawal symptoms from disabling him became too expensive. He started crossing Austin Boulevard regularly to buy heroin. It was easy to find and much cheaper than the Vicodin and OxyContin that he bought from the kids at school. At first, Jake would snort or smoke the heroin he bought, but as it happens with so many addicts, he eventually needed to feel the heat of the high faster and with more intensity. This is what pushed Jake past the fear of needles that used to make him cry in the doctor's office and eventually led to him taking the drug intravenously. For heroin addicts, this is often the point of no return.

Over the next few years and until I met Jake in his final stint in rehab that fall, he had checked into six different treatment programs. Jake's parents had money and good insurance, so he was afforded the best care possible. I only knew him for a month or so near the end of his life, but I can tell you that Jake took his recovery quite seriously. He was open, honest, and vulnerable. And he approached the therapy and treatment process with a sense of urgency that suggested to me that he understood the gravity of the situation. Unfortunately, none of that was enough to keep Jake from going out to buy that fentanyl-laced bag of heroin on the night before his twentieth birthday, maybe as some sort of celebration. Nobody will ever know.

A LETTER TO THE LOVED ONES OF ADDICTS AND ALCOHOLICS EVERYWHERE

I started receiving emails, texts, and phone calls within days of my return from the inpatient treatment facility where I went when there was finally nowhere else for me to go. Most of these emails were full of love, encouragement, concern, and support. But there was another group of people reaching out to me who were asking for my help.

I learned right away that my public stint in rehab, along with my history as a teacher and mentor, made me a potential lifeline for the people in my inner circle who may have loved ones suffering through addiction or alcoholism. I will never feel truly qualified or completely comfortable providing advice to anyone who decides to reach out to me for help with a loved one. But I will never stop trying.

I was particularly anxious and uncomfortable with this when I was just beginning my own journey in recovery. Technically, helping others is the twelfth and final step. And there is a good rationale behind the order of the steps. But I could never resist the urge to at least give it a shot, even in my first few months out of rehab. Over the years, I've fine-tuned the standard advice I have given to the loved ones of addicts and alcoholics who have reached out to me, and I've learned to create some clear boundaries when I do try to help. I know too many stories about addicts in early recovery who were pulled back into the depths of their addiction due to their kindhearted attempts to help other addicts who were struggling in one way or another. More than one counselor or therapist has warned me that I am especially at risk for that harmful outcome. It has been a pretty clear and consistent pattern in my adult life. I managed to resist the urge to try to rescue other addicts during the first few years of my recovery,

A LETTER

but I always tried to lend a hand to friends and families of other addicts who asked for my help. It never led me back to a bad place, and it definitely helped me get past a bit of the guilt and shame I felt surrounding the pain and suffering I had caused for my own loved ones over the years.

After boiling it down to what I consider to be the essentials and keeping it as simple as I possibly could, this is the general advice I still respond with when someone first contacts me in a moment of desperation, seeking help in their efforts to save the life of a person they love. Maybe including it here will help someone else who feels like all hope is lost. Nothing would make me happier.

> Dear all past, present, and future loved ones of an addict or alcoholic,
>
> Addiction is universally recognized in the medical community as a chronic brain disease. The good news is that it is diagnosable and treatable. The possibility of remission and recovery for people diagnosed with this insidious disease continues to increase over time. But the sad truth is that addiction also causes more collateral damage to families and loved ones than anyone could possibly know unless they had personal experience facing it head-on.

I will give you as much advice as I can conjure. But as you probably know, there is no plan of action for you or for the addict in your life that is sure to get everyone on the road to recovery. On the other hand, I have learned a great deal through my own difficult and ongoing battle with addiction. I have been lucky enough to receive both inpatient and outpatient treatment for my disease. And my recovery has still been slow and rocky. I am extremely proud of how far I've come, but I am not an expert. And I do not have it all figured out. I still have very real struggles of my own, but I have gained some valuable insight and perspective along the way that I hope will be helpful to you and your family. At the very least, it should help you understand that you are not alone and that all hope is not lost.

I'll start by telling you this. You must not underestimate the gravity of this moment. There is no danger in treating things as if they are worse than they are. However, there could be devastating consequences if you treat addiction or alcoholism too lightly, like something you can get under control, manage, or cure. You can be sure that, outward appearances aside, the addict or alcoholic you care about has already tried everything imaginable to get themselves under control. They don't want to drink or use drugs anymore. In fact, they hate it. But they are powerless over

A LETTER

drugs or alcohol. They are not weak. They are sick. It's a disease, remember. Like diabetes and brain cancer. And it cannot be cured or managed with willpower, tough love, medication, ultimatums, or money. And it certainly won't get better if it's avoided, ignored, or dismissed...although that option definitely is appealing right now, I'm sure. And I understand why it is the option most families and loved ones try first and often stick with to the bitter end.

I am going to give you a list of suggestions in no particular order. Keep in mind that these are only recommendations, and I am not a doctor or a licensed addiction counselor. But every one of these suggestions is based on my lived experience over the last ten years or so. I hope that what I've learned through that experience will also help you on your journey. You've taken the first and most important step by asking for help. Don't stop there. If you have any questions, please ask them. I am more than willing to listen, explain, and discuss.

- All of you should attend an Al-Anon meeting soon. Then, whatever your experience is, go to at least one more meeting before you decide if it's for you. Maybe shop around until you find a group where you feel comfortable.

- Remember the three Cs:
    - You didn't Cause it.
    - You can't Control it.
    - You can't Cure it.

- Show the addict in your life all the love and concern you can muster. Remember that they are sick. Remind them that you are worried about them, you are here for them, and you love them unconditionally.

- But…detach with love. Do not insert yourself into the addict's life in an attempt to heal them. It doesn't work, and it could backfire completely. But most importantly, you will become as sick as they are.

- Do not ignore the drug use, drinking, lying, or isolation of the addict in your life. Let them know, in a non-judgmental and non-confrontational way, that they're not getting away with it. Be specific when you discuss their behavior. Do not make assumptions or accusations or use words like always and never.

- Expect the addict in your life to get defensive and isolate themselves.

A LETTER

- Do not argue with the addict in your life. They're not thinking rationally. Even if they aren't drunk or high at the moment.

- It's perfectly acceptable for you not to trust the addict in your life. You can tell them why if you think it would help. But, again, it is important to be specific when talking about past behavior.

- Don't push the addict in your life. This could initiate their fight-or-flight response, and both of those options make the steps towards recovery much less likely.

- The addict in your life already knows they're sick, but they will have a very hard time admitting it to anyone because, as soon as they do, the wheels will be in motion for them to get treatment. And the addict in them desperately wants to continue drinking or using drugs despite any and all of the negative consequences they will have to endure.

- The addict in your life probably can't just cut back, or take a break, or learn to drink or use drugs in moderation. They have most likely tried all three of these strategies countless times, and things only got worse.

- Whatever you think you know about how much and how often the addict in your life is drinking or using drugs, you probably don't know half of it. And you probably never will. They're trying very hard to hide it from you. And they've gotten really good at it.

- The addict in your life will not just check themselves into rehab. If they say that they will, don't believe them. They're just buying time. If there are plans to begin treatment, try not to leave them alone for too long while they anxiously wait for their check-in time. I've heard too many terrible stories about what addicts and alcoholics do on the eve of treatment.

- Make sure the addict in your life knows that you will be there to support them if and when they decide that they are ready to do the work necessary to get clean and sober. This might be the most important piece of advice I have for you.

A LETTER

- Recovery is not linear. It's important for you to know that relapse is part of recovery for almost every addict or alcoholic who has ever tried to quit. Addicts in recovery try to value progress over perfection. Respond with kindness and love when the addict in your life relapses. Do not give up on them. Ask if there is anything you can do to help get their recovery back on track.

- There are several amazing and effective inpatient and outpatient treatment programs only a short plane ride away, at the very most. And the time for the addict in your life to get the appropriate treatment is now. Each day, their disease gets a little worse and kills them a little more. Tomorrow will be even more difficult than today.

Again, I don't have all the answers, but I do know what has and hasn't worked for me and what has and hasn't worked for countless other addicts and alcoholics. We are all different, but the symptoms, patterns, and general cycle of addiction and recovery are almost identical for all of us.

If you only take away one thing from what you've just read, please remember that if this disease goes untreated, it can only end with jails, institutions, or death. It needs to be treated and monitored continuously for the rest of the addict's life.

But the good news is that if the disease is treated, monitored, and managed, the addict in your life can live a long, rich, and fulfilling life. The twelve steps really do work if you work them. Almost without exception.

There is still hope for you and for the addict you love.

ANNE PIACCINI
AN ASSISTANT STATE'S ATTORNEY

After I was released on bond, but before my next appearance in court, I met with my lawyers and my brother to discuss the judge and the assistant state's attorney assigned to my case. This was when I first learned how significant and sometimes fate-sealing this phase of a defendant's criminal case can be. Understandably, I had no say in who would be prosecuting my case, and I can only theorize about how that decision was made. Still, I did have some limited legal options regarding the judge that would hear my case. The lawyers on my team had already decided that we shouldn't object to the judge we drew, but everyone was anxious to discuss all of the gathered intel on the prosecutor who would be making the most important decisions regarding what the remainder of my life would look like.

Cook County Assistant State's Attorney, Anne Piaccini, lived in the community where I grew up and where I was living with my family at the time of my offense. I imagine she laid her head on her pillow every night only a matter of blocks from the school where I had been teaching for the last ten years. I wonder if this kind of proximity and familiarity had any impact on the way Ms. Piaccini felt about me or my case. Like most public schools in America, the public schools in Oak Park are funded, in large part, by property tax dollars. And some of those tax dollars were used to pay my salary, even after I was put on administrative leave during the criminal investigation and eventual prosecution of the crimes I was charged with. I wonder if Ms. Piaccini thought about this as my case made its way through the Cook County Criminal Courts.

Not long after prosecuting my case, Ms. Piaccini was elected to serve as a municipal judge in Cook County. Her motivation for this career change is unknown to me, and I haven't read anything about any of the cases she has presided over in her new role, but as an assistant state's attorney, Ms. Piacccini had the reputation of being tough and fair. These are two adjectives of high praise for any attorney in her position, no doubt. She had been prosecuting sex crimes for years, and it was clear that she took this very important job seriously.

I was only in the same room with Ms. Piaccini seven or eight times during the year that she was prosecuting my case. She usually stood about four feet away from me for approximately five minutes during each of my appearances in court. She often wore some kind of dark pantsuit with a pair of white sneakers. And it seemed like she spent most of her day running from courtroom to courtroom in that scary, old courthouse at the corner of 26th and California. Ms. Piaccini never made eye contact with me, but for some reason, I always hoped she would.

I often wondered how Ms. Piaccini dealt with the undeniable weight that came with the responsibility of being an assistant state's attorney. The average person who hasn't had any experience in the criminal justice system probably doesn't comprehend the power and influence of the state's prosecutors. It's only normal for people to assume that the judge and the jury *are* the proverbial judge and jury of most criminal cases. And although judges and juries certainly have the final say in the fate of some defendants, so much of what will become of them has been decided well before a judge or jury even enters the picture. On top of that, the vast majority of criminal cases result in plea deals of some kind or another. Courtroom trials are the exception, not the rule.

Once the police completed their criminal investigation into the allegations made against me, no single person or entity was more responsible in determining the outcome of my case than Ms. Piaccini and the Office of the State's Attorney. And I was just one of the countless manilla folders stacked precariously on the wobbly, plastic cart that Ms. Piaccini pushed around the courthouse all day. Each of those folders carried the name of a human being with a unique and complicated story, a human being with a family, a human being with an impossible-to-measure potential and an unknown probability for rehabilitation and redemption. I can only guess how much time Ms. Piaccini had to decide what kind of chance she would give to each of the defendants whose names were written on those folders stacked up in front of her. But the height of that stack suggested to me that her caseload didn't allow her to give each one of them the kind of thought and energy she would've liked to give them. Not to mention how difficult it must've been for Ms. Piaccini to determine the relevance and significance of any mitigating factors involved in the crimes they allegedly committed.

Once Ms. Piaccini received the final report from the detectives who investigated my case, she first had to decide whether there was enough evidence to justify any criminal charges. This decision wasn't about whether she thought I committed any crimes, but whether there would be enough evidence to convince a judge or jury beyond a reasonable doubt that I had broken the law. State's Attorney offices are not in the business of pursuing criminal charges in cases that they think they might lose, especially in a case like mine—one that would be on the news. It could be a chance for some public recognition if she could put away a semi-public figure for sexually abusing a minor, but I'm guessing they would not want to face the scrutiny that would've come with failing to secure a conviction in a case like mine.

I can't imagine many jobs more difficult, depressing, or disheartening than being an assistant state's attorney in charge of prosecuting sex crimes. Although, it must've been incredibly rewarding when the hard work paid off, and the system worked and justice was finally served in one of the many truly disturbing cases that Ms. Piaccini handled during her time in that role. It's no secret that many sexual assaults and other sex crimes go altogether unreported. And there are any number of understandable explanations for that. But maybe even more alarming and telling is the great number of sex crimes that are reported but do not result in a conviction of any kind.

For obvious reasons, victims of sex crimes are sometimes reluctant to testify in court. This fact, along with a number of other factors unique to crimes like these, makes sex offenses some of the most difficult cases to prosecute successfully. On the other hand, relatively speaking, my case was kind of a slam dunk for Ms. Piaccini. Although it didn't end exactly how she would've liked it to, I'm guessing, the eventual felony conviction must have brought her some level of satisfaction, especially considering the public nature of the charges against me. And as crazy as this sounds, in some strange way, I was satisfied too. Obviously, the outcome could've been much worse for me. In the end, I was spared any prison time, but the judge did sentence me to two years of sex offender probation, mandatory sex offender therapy, and a lifetime sex offender registration. And from that point forward, I would be classified as a felon and a "sexual predator" by the state of Illinois. But deep down, I was glad that I didn't get away with it. I was convicted of a crime I committed. And in that sense, the system worked the way it was designed to work, I think. And I accept that.

I waited exactly one year to learn my fate, most of it on house arrest, in rehab, or with a therapist. And I spent a lot of that time wondering about the process that Ms. Piaccini went through when deciding which charges to pursue or what kind of plea deals to offer the people she prosecuted. Did she use some kind of system to evaluate each case, like the rubrics I used to grade student essays about *Great Expectations*? Or did she just trust her gut instinct? How much weight did she give to the wishes of the victims? Was she ever influenced by the reputation of the defense lawyer she was facing? Did she ever disagree with the decisions her bosses made regarding the cases she prosecuted? How did race factor into how she prosecuted her cases? Did she ever look back and second guess any of her decisions? Was it possible for her to get in her car and drive home every night without taking any of the names written on those manilla folders with her? What about the names of the victims? Did she carry with her the sad and disturbing truths she learned from the victims in her cases? Or was she able to just punch in and punch out like a factory worker? Was she honest with her family and friends about it when they asked her how things were at work? Did she have sympathy for any of the people she was prosecuting? Did she think the criminal justice system was fair and reasonable? Did she trust the police officers who investigated the crimes she prosecuted? Did she believe that prison was the best and most appropriate consequence for the people she told judges and juries to send there? Did she wish she could do more?

I bet these are the same kind of questions my dad would ask an assistant state's attorney over a few glasses of good Italian wine. And I'm sure that Ms. Piaccini's responses to questions like these would be complicated, interesting, and worth collecting.

CARL MASON
MY PROBATION OFFICER

After I made my way through the metal detector and checked in at the front desk for my first appointment with my probation officer, I took a seat on a bench in the crowded lobby and waited anxiously for my name to be called. As was the norm for all of my experiences at the time, I had no idea what to expect. I was in a completely unfamiliar environment, and nothing I had been through in my life to that point had prepared me for the moment I was living.

I was dressed in khakis and a button-down shirt (I couldn't have looked more like an English teacher), and I was carrying a binder containing all of the documents given to me in court a few days earlier, when I was convicted of aggravated criminal sexual abuse and sentenced to two years of sex offender probation. I was the only White person in sight, and nobody else was wearing khakis.

The waiting room was clean and quiet, and it was hard to ignore the skunky weed stench hanging in the air. The other probationers were looking at me with not-so-subtle curiosity. Finally, the guy sitting next to me leaned in and asked me if I was a lawyer. I laughed awkwardly and told him that, like him, I was in fact here to see my probation officer. And I'll never forget his response. He said, "Damn, what happened? You beat your girl's ass or something?" After another awkward laugh, I replied, "Nah, man, I just got caught up in some shit." This is what my lawyer told me to say when anyone asked me what I was in for. It must've worked, because my bench mate then busted out in laughter and said, "Oh, yeah, I feel ya, brother. We all got caught up in some shit. What was it, cocaine?" I winked at him and said, "Something like that." We high-fived and laughed together until the lady behind the desk told us, much like I was told by most of my teachers in high school, that she would "put us out" if we didn't knock it off. My new friend looked at me and whispered, "Man, fuck her. Who she think she is?" But neither of us said another word.

Finally, my probation officer appeared at the front desk. And after gossiping with the receptionist for a few minutes, he turned around, looked right at me, and said in a deep baritone voice, "Come with me, Mr. Lind." I remember that he was smiling. And that definitely put me at ease as I approached him with my hand out. He seemed a little surprised as he shook my hand and I motioned for him to lead the way. But he insisted that I walk ahead of him. I asked him about this later, and he told me that, as a safety measure, he was trained to never put his back to one of his "clients." We eventually made our way to his cubicle in the back, and he told me to have a seat in the cushioned chair directly across from his desk.

Officer Mason reminded me of one of my favorite Chicago Bears players of all time. He looked like Mike Singletary... if Mike Singletary never worked out or played football. He was stout with strong shoulders and giant hands, but his kind eyes and easy smile offset anything intimidating about his appearance. He was probably in his early fifties, and he was almost always dressed the same, jeans and an oversized sweater. I once made a joke about his "Cosby sweater," but Officer Mason didn't laugh.

I spent about two hours signing papers, going over the rules and procedures of my probation, and answering Officer Mason's questions that day, but I walked out of my first official probation meeting with renewed optimism. I started to believe that the next two years might not be as unbearable as I had imagined. From the very start, Officer Mason treated me with respect, and he never made assumptions about my case or my life. It was immediately clear that he was a good man who understood that each of his clients had a story and that he needed to manage each of our cases differently depending on that story.

It reminded me of how I always tried to approach teaching. It was my philosophy to meet each student where they were, and the more I knew about them, the better I could adjust my teaching to meet their needs. During one of my later meetings with Officer Mason, as I was expressing the guilt and shame I felt about the pain and suffering I had caused through my careless and irresponsible behavior, he stopped me, started slowly shaking his head, and said, "Mr. Lind, what you did is like a two." Sometimes, I repeat that sentence over and over in my head when I'm having an especially bad day. It will never feel like a two to me, but at least it doesn't feel like a ten anymore.

Over time, I learned bits and pieces of Officer Mason's story. Sometimes, he would just offer it up, but most of the time, it was the result of my carefully thought-out conversation starters. I came to consider it my mission to learn more about him, but it wasn't easy. Officer Mason usually had no interest in chatting with me, and I didn't want to upset him. But I knew he had a story, too, and I desperately wanted to hear it. Pretty early on, I managed to learn that Officer Mason still lived in the West Side neighborhood where he grew up. As it turns out, Officer Mason and I had spent most of our lives within a mile or two of each other. He lived not too far on the other side of that invisible wall that separated Oak Park from the West Side of Chicago. The resources and opportunities were far more plentiful on my side of that wall, but my geographic luck and undeniable privilege weren't enough to keep me out of Officer Mason's cubicle in the Cook County Adult Probation Department. And I don't think the irony of our relationship was lost on either of us. I was a White, suburban, convicted felon reporting to my hard-working, dedicated, Black probation officer, who grew up on the West Side. I desperately wanted to ask Officer Mason what he thought about it all, but I decided against it. And I will always regret that.

I met with Officer Mason once a week for almost two years, and he and his partner came to my apartment once a month or so to make sure I wasn't violating any of the conditions of my probation. Those meetings and home visits shouldn't have been much of an inconvenience, but there were periods of time when they left me crippled with anxiety. My old fear of being exposed was showing its face again, and this time, I had a very real reason to be scared.

I relapsed twice on probation and began using cocaine again. And even under the best circumstances, the paranoia can be debilitating during a binge. After being spared any time in prison for the felonies I was originally charged with, I was risking it all again...and again. In both situations, I knew I was going to get caught and knew the potential consequences for that, but it still wasn't enough to make me stop. Here's the sad truth: as soon as I decided to give cocaine another chance to destroy me, I was powerless again and needed to find yet another rock bottom if I was ever truly going to clean up my act. So, after sweating it out and passing several drug tests, it was still inevitable that I would eventually push my luck and get caught. But both times this happened to me, Officer Mason was honest, compassionate, and understanding with me. He definitely didn't let it slide, but he didn't talk down to me or berate me for lying to him or violating the terms of my probation. On both occasions, he filed probation violations with the court, and I'm grateful that he did.

Fortunately for me, after testing positive for cocaine use twice, the judge was satisfied with my decision to check back into an outpatient treatment program. And that was definitely what I needed. As long as I successfully completed twenty weeks of rehab and didn't have any more failed drug tests, the probation violations against me would be dismissed.

Once I was back in rehab and committed to my sobriety and recovery again, seeing Officer Mason no longer gave any cause for anxiety or concern. In truth, I looked forward to seeing him at our weekly meetings. And I was sad and disappointed when, a few months before my probation was successfully terminated, Officer Mason was suddenly reassigned to a different unit. I ended up with a new probation officer, who was quite nice, too, but there wasn't enough time to learn much about her story. And I never got the chance to say goodbye to or thank Officer Mason for treating me with respect, listening to my story, and doing his best to support me as I stumbled my way through a very difficult time of my life.

MY DAD

Sometime during my junior year in high school, I ran away from home with only the clothes on my back and a couple of twenties I stole off of my dad's dresser while he was in the shower a day or two earlier. I am unsure of the exact date of this particular incident, but it seems to me that it was sometime after I was removed from the gifted program at school, but before I was impeached from the student council. I do know that it was during the regrettable stage of my adolescence in which I was most despicable. The boneheaded and drunk teenager who pushed past my dad and out the front door that night is someone I dream about going back in time to shake…and maybe to sit down with and talk to for a few hours. Over the years, it has become more and more clear why my dad used to rather frequently remind me that I was being a "dickhead." I think that was probably too kind.

It must've been a weekend because I remember that I went to a party earlier in the night. And, as was common practice for me back then, I came home several hours late and pretty drunk. Out of pure frustration and lack of new ideas, my parents were left with few options when I stumbled into their room to tell them I was home. But on this night, I must've been especially rude or unintelligible because an argument ensued.

As I remember it, my dad took the lead on this one. And although the details are obviously a bit foggy, I remember threatening to climb out of my second-floor bedroom window if my dad wouldn't let me leave. I made this threat because the argument had gotten to a point where my dad had pulled up a chair outside of my room to make sure I wouldn't attempt to escape into the darkness. The potential danger of me falling from my bedroom window in the middle of the night must've softened my dad's stance a bit, and he stepped aside just enough for me to get through the door. And off I went. I can't even imagine what the conversation between my mom

MY DAD

and dad must have been like after I left. I hope it was a simple "good riddance," but I doubt it was that simple.

I spent approximately two weeks on the run from reality. At the time, I remember considering it a great success, and I wore my rebellion on my chest like a badge of honor. But it would be impossible to express how guilty and ashamed I feel about it today. I started feeling that way a day or two after my return, and it only grew over time. The truth was that I hated myself back then.

While I was away from home, my mom had pretty serious surgery. I had final exams. I got drunk nearly every day. And I didn't call home once. I bounced from house to house of friends who had sympathetic parents, but obviously, I couldn't do that forever. And after a couple of weeks, I ran out of money and willing innkeepers. It was time to hang my head, put my tail between my legs, and go home. I remember the fear and anxiety I felt as I walked toward my house that day. I didn't know what to expect when I walked through the front door, but I was pretty sure it wasn't going to be good. Little did I know.

Nobody replied to my whimpered, "Hello?" as I closed the front door behind me, but I could hear the sound of my parents talking in the kitchen. I made my way slowly through the dining room, and as I crossed the threshold into the kitchen,

I saw my dad at the sink, doing some dishes. My mom was sitting at the kitchen table in the breakfast area to my right. They were still unaware that I was home.

This is one of those moments that I can recreate in my mind's eye without even thinking. I can see the light coming through the windows from the backyard. I can make out each of the little black and white flooring tiles. And I can hear the water running from the faucet and into the sink. I suppose the mental imprint of that moment has survived this long, untouched and unfaded, because, at that moment, I was utterly convinced that my life was about to get a lot worse and that maybe I'd never recover. Also, I was feeling a whole new level of shame that I had never experienced before. What I didn't know at the time was that I would have a very similar experience about twenty-five years later. Although the two situations seem to be much different on the surface, the feelings I experienced in each case were eerily similar. When I opened the door of my brother's car in front of the first precinct police station and got out to cross the busy street to turn myself in on felony sex offense charges, I was instantly reminded of the way I felt standing in the doorway of my kitchen that day, waiting for my parents to notice that I had returned from my ill-advised two-week absence from home.

MY DAD

My second "hello" was loud enough for both of my parents to hear. My dad made a quick turnaround, and it took me a second to realize and process the fact that he was holding a big knife. Then, it took me another few seconds to rid myself of the fear that he might use that big knife to teach me a lesson about what happens to kids with two hard-working, loving, and compassionate parents who run away from home for two weeks for no good reason. Kids who don't even call home when one of those hard-working, loving, and compassionate parents is in the hospital having a serious surgery. But, against all odds and probably his natural instinct, my dad set the big knife down and smiled. And my mom got up from her seat at the kitchen table. And both of them approached me with outstretched arms. And they hugged me. I'm sure I was crying, but I'm guessing there were some tears in their eyes too. When the group hug came to an end, my dad said, "Welcome back. I'm glad you're home. Call your friends. Tell them to come over. I'll make ribs."

My dad's ribs were my favorite meal. They still are. I regularly use his recipe for the dry rub and the barbeque sauce to make ribs for my birthday, my sons' birthdays, and other special occasions. It is an understatement of great magnitude to say that I was more than a little surprised by my dad's reaction and response when I returned home that day. Although I was mildly suspicious that what he was setting up was some kind of last supper situation, I didn't ask any questions. I made some calls, and he made the ribs. A few of my friends (who were also a little nervous) came over, and we had a nice dinner. It was as if my great transgression had just disappeared into the ether.

I didn't talk to either of my parents about the day I came home, or the two weeks I was gone, for several more years. I think I was scared to jinx it or something. And I'm not sure what instigated the conversation when it finally happened, but I do remember bringing it up to my dad one night at the farm years later. As usual, we were all drinking good Italian wine around the dinner table after finishing some elaborate and delicious meal my parents concocted and prepared together. And I reminded my mom and dad, along with whomever else was at the farm that night, what happened when I ran away from home back in high school and, more importantly, what happened when I came home. Then I remember asking my dad why he responded the way he did. And he just smiled a little and said that he just didn't want me to leave again. I went on to ask him if, even for an instant, he considered making good use of the knife he had in his hand when he first turned around to see me standing there. And he smiled again, but this time he didn't answer.

SCOTT
A SEX OFFENDER THERAPIST

Scott was in his sixties. He was White, kind of puffy, and his dyed-blonde hair was obvious and not flattering. But he possessed the kind of self-deprecating sense of humor that felt genuine to me. He had been providing therapy to convicted sex offenders in Illinois for more than twenty years when I first met him. And he complained a lot. But I could tell that he loved his job. Scott took pride in helping this unfortunately qualified population of men, and he really did believe that he was helping. Most of the time, he was. Other times he could be demeaning, insensitive, rude, or deliberately intimidating...kind of like a playground bully.

I arrived for my first individual session with Scott not knowing what to expect. I was scared and fairly certain that it wasn't going to be anything like the therapy I had grown accustomed to, the kind of therapy I was first introduced to in high school, when my battle with guilt, shame, and self-hate began. My meetings with Scott weren't going to be as comfortable as my weekly sessions with the therapist I had been seeing since I first became concerned about how I was coping with my dad's sudden and terminal illness. The summer camp, sing-along, "Tell me how that makes you feel" therapy from my drug rehab programs was also just right for me, and it worked, but I had a feeling that court-ordered sex offender therapy wouldn't have quite the same vibe. And there is no way I could've anticipated how challenging, uncomfortable, scary, and sometimes soul-crushing my experience in those dreaded Tuesday evening sessions could be, especially in the beginning.

When I showed up for my first appointment, Scott immediately launched into a cold and stern lecture, not unlike the ones I eventually came to expect from him. I don't recall exactly what he said, but his general message seemed to be that he didn't trust me and that he knew precisely what I was

SCOTT

going to say and how I was going to behave. It was Scott's way of telling me that he expected me to lie about my offense, to refuse to take appropriate responsibility for my actions, and to minimize the impact that my deviant and illegal behavior had on my victim and my family. It was clear that he was looking forward to exposing me when I would inevitably try to pull one over on him. And it seemed like he couldn't wait to call me out and force me to face the facts after catching me in the act. In effect, Scott was extending his bat toward the left-field bleachers in Yankee Stadium, like Babe Ruth calling his shot in the World Series. Not only did he prematurely announce the fact that he would win, Scott presented me with his entire game plan in our very first session.

I nodded politely and took notes as Scott continued to assert his dominance, but I could feel myself getting defensive. This therapist, who was supposed to be helping me, called me a liar before I even said a word. But I've read enough books and been to enough twelve-step meetings to know that my reaction to this didn't have much to do with him. I had been lying to everyone, including myself, for years, and I hated myself for it. Who was he to so accurately measure my character before taking the time to get to know me? Needless to say, Scott's approach to my therapy struck a nerve, and I felt the resentment expanding inside of me like a balloon filled with broken glass. I almost immediately despised him. And for a few weeks, it only got worse.

I had to complete three tasks before my second meeting with Scott. But before I began my first homework assignment, I devised a vengeful plan to defeat him. By the time I was done with Scott, he would be dejected and full of remorse for daring to read me based on whatever basic and misleading information he had in some manilla folder with my name on it. My initial instinct was to prove that I could indeed fool him, but I decided instead to kill him with kindness, honesty, and willingness to listen and actively engage in my therapy. I would even try to respect Scott.

My first assignment was to complete a packet of questions, mostly about the offense that landed me in sex offender therapy. This was my chance to prove that Scott was wrong about me. I knew what he was expecting, so I answered every question with brutal honesty. I resisted any urge to minimize, shift blame, or leave out any of the difficult and embarrassing details of what I had done. I even included parts of the story that I knew Scott wouldn't find in the police report or any of the other court documents he had. There were damning details that never came out, but I put it all on the table that day. And I didn't make excuses or ignore the devastation that my behavior left behind. But I also reported that outside of the offense that I was charged with and eventually convicted of, I had never had any kind of sexual contact or engaged in any kind of sexually inappropriate behavior with any of my students or anyone else under the legal age of consent. I knew he wouldn't believe that, but it was the truth, and I was prepared for him to challenge me on it in therapy. And after about six months of individual and group therapy with Scott, I would be given the chance to prove it. I just didn't know that yet.

The other two tasks I was required to do before my initial assessment could be finalized were "diagnostic tests" to be completed in a dirty, windowless room adjacent to Scott's office. The first of these tests had hundreds of multiple-choice questions about deviant sexual behaviors, human anatomy, gender roles, and morality, among other things. I felt as if my brain was going to break through my skull as I struggled to determine the purpose of each and every question I answered. This assessment took about four hours to complete...about the same amount of time it took me to finish the SAT in 1992. The second "test" wasn't anything I had anticipated, and I will never forget the way it made me feel.

After collecting my scantron from the first test, Scott sat me down in a folding chair in front of some ancient computer that was making noises indicating that it might need a tune-up. He told me to listen carefully as he explained the directions. It was clear to me that many of Scott's previous clients had tainted the results of this assessment because they didn't pay attention to him. His face was turning red as he preemptively scolded me for screwing it up. This is what my second assessment entailed: First, I had to view a collection of images featuring people of all ages, races, and genders. Using the mouse, I would have five seconds to look at each image, imagine having sex with the person in the image, then rate my resulting sexual arousal. My "score" would be based in part on the speed in which I gave my rating. Scott explained how the five-second rule would uncover any deception I may or may not be planning. Again, he was implying that I was a liar. Needless to say, I was confused and anxious. I wanted to get this over with and get out of his office, but I was determined to take it seriously. I needed to stick to my plan.

So for the next hour, I looked at dozens of pictures of adults and children in various stages of undress. Their facial expressions and body language were confusing and troubling. And I had five seconds to report the level of my sexual arousal when imagining having sex with each photographed person... and lots of them were children. There were tears in my eyes within minutes of beginning this process. And I could feel myself getting physically ill. I managed to stay in the chair

SCOTT

long enough to get through all the pictures, but it was traumatizing, and I do not use that word without forethought.

When that terrible slide show was over, and all of my responses were recorded, I knocked on the door of Scott's office and let him know I was finished. He shook my hand and told me he'd see me the following week. I didn't say anything. And I managed to hold back the tears until I got to my car. Then I immediately called my mom and let it all out. I felt like I had just been part of some unethical, psychological experiment, and I couldn't stand the thought of coming back to that office every week for the next eighteen months.

My next individual session with Scott was intense. He spent most of the hour explaining his analysis of the three assessments I had completed the week before. And he stated his opinions regarding those results as if they were facts. Scott was pleased to report that I had healthy beliefs about gender and an acceptable understanding of the female body. He told me that many of his clients lacked the most basic knowledge about women and their bodies. It seemed inappropriate for him to tell me this, but I would learn over time that it was not uncommon for Scott to gossip about his other clients. He then praised me for my attention to detail in answering the questions about my offense, but he also made it clear to me that he knew I was lying about that being my only sexual contact with a minor. He told me that in his twenty-plus years as a therapist for sex offenders, he didn't have a single client who was arrested after the first and only time he acted on his deviant, sexual impulses.

Scott went on to say that I was not the first client to deny it and that I would have to confess to all of my other illegal sexual activities if I intended to complete my treatment successfully. Again, I was prepared for this, and I calmly repeated the truth. I told Scott that I understood why he was making that assumption, and I didn't disregard his many years of experience. But I also let him know that I was an exception to the pattern of behavior that he had observed in his practice. That's when Scott told me about the mandatory polygraph exams. He said he couldn't wait for me to fail.

Scott's analysis of my sexual interest assessment results proved to be something that we could mostly agree on. He informed me that my "score" indicated that my sexual interest was "in the range of normal." And I'm not going to lie, as much as I despised the particular assessment tool, I was happy to hear a qualified expert tell me that I was not some sick and deviant pervert. Of course, I already knew that about myself, but the next eighteen months of therapy would've been a lot harder if Scott didn't agree. But I did point out to Scott how inappropriate and flawed I thought that assessment was, not to mention how traumatic it was for me to take. And Scott responded by telling me not to worry about it. My results were "in the range of normal." I reminded him that I understood that but that I still had a problem with how the assessment was administered. I told him that I thought it was unnecessarily traumatic, potentially unethical, and probably ineffective in diagnosing sexual deviance if that was, indeed, the assessment's intended purpose. I realized right there that I was arguing with him about the accuracy of an assessment tool that just assessed me as "in the range of normal," but I just couldn't help myself. We went back and forth for about twenty minutes before I started to get emotional, and Scott chastised me for challenging his expertise and professional opinion. At that point, he told me that I needed to adjust my attitude before I returned the next week.

I drove home angry after my second session with Scott, and I couldn't shake the thought that this experience was going to be torturous and possibly even counterproductive. But I was going to have to show up and deal with it every week for at least eighteen months. There was no way around that. But I wasn't sure that I could maintain an open mind and a positive attitude as I had originally planned to do.

Over the next few months, though, Scott and I slowly worked through our issues. We definitely butted heads every now and then, but as I continued to prove to him that I was taking every assignment seriously and being an active leader in our group sessions, he began to treat me almost as his intern or something. And this made me uncomfortable at times. It was not uncommon for Scott to take a subtle jab at one of the other men in the group before glancing over at me like I was somehow complicit in his little inside jokes. It seemed that I was the one client he treated as his peer, and this was only because I was educated, White, paid attention to current events, and was relatively well-spoken and comfortable in social interactions. This combination of personality traits and life experience wasn't all that common in the group. And Scott's seemingly preferential treatment of me sometimes resulted in the other guys in the group resenting me, I think, like students who roll their eyes at the teacher's pet. The uncomfortable truth was that I wanted to be on both teams. And that was a struggle I continued to face but never truly resolved.

The turning point in my relationship with Scott finally occurred during the individual session that followed my sexual history polygraph. As he announced to me during my very first session six months earlier, this was going to be his chance to break me down and make me face the truth. According to Scott, this was the only way I could do the real work that I needed to do to complete my court-ordered sex offender therapy successfully. I had been looking forward to this day just as much as Scott had been. It was going to be my chance to show him that I didn't fit into the box he had made for me, the box he built over twenty-plus years of counseling convicted sex offenders.

It was true, more true than I originally believed it to be, that I did have a lot in common with the other men in my group, but I was also different. I did not fit the pattern or live up to the stereotype that follows all convicted sex offenders. This didn't make me any less guilty than any of the rest of them, and it certainly didn't make me a better person, but it did make Scott wrong about *me*. I walked into his office a few days after passing my polygraph exam, tossed my coat onto the cabinet next to the fake fern, sat down in the dusty, old chair, and smiled at him. I knew he had already received the official report from the polygraph administrator. And I was sure that he had already read the section informing him that my responses to all three relevant questions showed no evidence of deception. On several occasions during my first six months of therapy, Scott pledged his unwavering support of polygraph testing as a treatment tool. And if he was going to take the negative results as fact, as he always did during my time working with him, he would also have to accept *my* results and adjust my therapy accordingly.

During my first six months of therapy with Scott, I had more than one dream of him issuing some long and detailed apology where he admitted that it was a mistake for him to make assumptions about my life before he had the benefit of getting to know me. And Scott earned my respect during that first session after my polygraph exam, when he basically did just that. And then he did it again later that night when we met as a group. Scott made sure to remind us all that he had never been wrong like this before, but he did admit that he *was* wrong. It took about six months, but Scott finally believed me. And now that he knew that the narrative I had been telling and retelling him was indeed the truth, the unnecessary tension between us could finally dissipate and no longer complicate the process for me. It made it much more likely that I would take something positive away from my therapy. I was finally free to grow and evolve, despite my initial skepticism and personal issues with Scott.

The final twelve months of my therapy with Scott were much better and more helpful than the first six months had been. I didn't exactly look forward to my weekly sessions, but I didn't dread them either. I did come to relish the few minutes the guys and I would have together in the room before Scott would show up. It was like a locker room full of misfits, but all of us were loveable in one way or another. And our emotional bond was undeniable, given what we had shared with each other as part of this process. We were a team. It was a team I never dreamed of being a part of, but it was a team, nonetheless.

Scott allowed us to bring treats for the group on our last day of therapy once we had finally checked all the boxes necessary to advance through all four levels of the curriculum that Scott and his colleagues had developed and fine-tuned over the years. During the course of my therapy, this treat-bringing tradition had become a kind of competition. It started with cookies, but the last few guys had really made a statement with their treat of choice. One of the men brought rib tips when he "graduated" a couple of weeks before I did.

I walked through the door with great pride on my last day, not just because I had survived and successfully completed my therapy but also because I was carrying a catering tray stacked with sandwiches. After I set down and unwrapped the tray of my favorite Italian subs, I told the rest of the guys to grab a plate and help themselves. I stood by the plates, and I was greeted with a warm hug from each of the men in my group before they helped themselves to the graduation feast. Some of them stopped and had a few nice words for me. And more than one of them seemed to be on the verge of tears. I'm sure the tears gathering in my eyes were visible to them too.

But we couldn't exchange phone numbers or make arrangements to see each other outside of that dank room. It was illegal for us to associate with each other, at least until we were off of probation. But even then, the law is vague and ambiguous at best. I knew this was the last time I would see any of these men. And even though I had always known that it made me sad.

After we were done literally breaking bread together during my final group session, I was given a chance to read a letter I had written to the other men in the group. Then they were given the chance to tell me what I'd meant to them as part of their process. Eventually, Scott would say a few words about me and my progress throughout therapy. And what he said was more thoughtful and kind than he'd ever been...but of course, he managed to take a few personal but funny shots at me too. I didn't expect anything less.

This is the kind of shit I have always lived for, people telling each other how they really feel, expressing genuine emotion and gratitude, especially men. I had a few experiences like this in my rehab environments, but this one reminded me more of the time I spent working with the Spoken Word Club when I was a teacher. It was like the final showcase we would put on near the end of the school year when the students and teachers would share memories and say farewell to the graduating seniors. But on my final day of sex offender therapy, in that dank room with ten other convicted sex offenders, I felt like both a teacher *and* a graduating student. My heart was heavy as I walked to my car and, once again, put my head in my hands and cried.

GRACE
A POLYGRAPH ADMINISTRATOR

I sat, drinking coffee and smoking (two things I had read that one shouldn't do before taking a polygraph test) on a short, brick wall outside of the office in which I was to take my sexual history polygraph. I spent most of the previous night panicking and pacing the perimeter of my apartment. I had been dreading this day for months. And it was finally here. In a matter of two or three hours, I would either be able to breathe a little easier or be facing an altogether new nightmare. I finished my second cigarette and gave myself a little pep talk before I walked through the double doors of a nondescript office at the end of a mini-mall in some forgettable suburb of Chicago. I remember thinking about how strange it would be to work at a place like this: to pull into that parking lot five days a week, walk through those doors, and administer detailed interviews and polygraph exams to convicted sex offenders and other criminals.

The woman who led me into the interview room in the back of the office was tall and White, maybe in her early sixties. Her name was Grace. I noticed a tattoo of a shooting star hiding beneath the straps of the sandal she wore on her right foot. And she wore some sort of orthopedic boot that extended almost to the knee of her left leg. Her straight brown hair extended past her waist. She greeted me with a gentle smile as we sat down across from each other. I would only see her smile one more time before I left her office. She then took out a well-worn binder and didn't waste any time before she started asking questions.

These were not the questions I'd be tested on when she would later connect me to the computer for the polygraph exam, but I did recognize most of them from the assessments I had taken on my second visit to Scott's office. Most of the questions were about my sexual behavior. Once again, I had

GRACE

to report that I hadn't had sex with any animals or dead bodies. Grace didn't change the expression on her face once during the first hour of my interview, but something happened shortly after she began a line of questioning about my past drug use and other risk-taking behavior.

As I told Grace the story of my ongoing battle with drug addiction, giving her more details than she was used to, I'm sure, I could see something changing in her face. And her shoulders dropped a little. And she started tapping her sandaled foot on the linoleum-tiled floor. I recognized that this sudden change in her demeanor could mean one of two things. She had either personally battled addiction to drugs or alcohol, or someone very close to her had been cursed with this insidious disease.

Eventually, Grace cracked and let down her guard long enough to let me in on some of her story. Her professional affect went out the window temporarily as she told me about her brother. He was a drug addict. And she told me how hard it had been for him and her family to deal with the seemingly endless sadness, anger, and disappointment that had followed her brother and his addiction everywhere he went for as long as she could remember. We both cried a little as we talked about how devastating and destructive addiction can be to entire families. She told me that I should be proud of myself for how hard I seemed to be working on my recovery. She went on to remind me that my whole family was suffering with me and that my recovery was just as important to them as it was to me. I nodded my head in silent agreement and thanked her before using one of my sleeves to wipe my eyes dry and hide my face for a minute. Then Grace started hooking me up to the machine.

Grace instructed me several times not to move at all during my polygraph exam. I was seated in a hard chair with my bent right arm resting on the desk next to me. There were electrodes strapped to my chest to monitor my heart rate and breathing. I also had some contraption connected to my right index finger that had something to do with biometrics, I think. I'm pretty sure it just measured how sweaty I got during the test. And finally, my feet were on some sort of plastic mat with sensors that would uncover any other efforts at deception. Needless to say, it wasn't very comfortable. And it was extremely difficult to remain perfectly still during the test.

The actual polygraph exam takes less than fifteen minutes, but I knew that if I moved or wiggled or twitched too much for Grace's liking, my test would be considered unreliable, and I'd have to explain to Scott why I was purposefully trying to throw off the results of the test. This only made it harder to stay still as Grace went through her routine. She started with a few baseline questions. Was this my name? Was it a Monday? Have I ever told a lie? Every question she asked should have a simple yes or no answer. The baseline questions were followed by three "relevant questions." All three of these questions were asking me the same thing in a different way. The one truly relevant question was, "Had I ever had any sexual contact with any other minors aside from the offense that I was convicted of?" In short, were there any other victims? As I responded, "No," as calmly as possible, I could feel my heart beating harder and faster. And it seemed like I could feel the sweat building under the contraption clipped to the end of my index finger. And I was sure that my breathing was getting faster and shallower by the second.

When Grace finally informed me that the test was complete, I was convinced that I had failed. I had been lying to so many people for so long. And I was sure that my residual anxiety, guilt, and shame still moved the needles on her machine. It didn't matter that I had answered all of her questions truthfully; I just knew that Grace was about to tell me that the results of my polygraph exam indicated unmistakable and unforgivable deceit. But after she sat staring at the monitor in front of her for what seemed like an hour, Grace flashed her second brief smile before she revealed that there were no signs of deception in any of my answers to the relevant questions. I'd like to think that Grace was rooting for me to pass, which I bet is an uncommon feeling in her line of work. I imagine that she usually takes pride in catching criminals and deviants in their lies.

After receiving the good news, I had an overwhelming desire to give Grace a big bear-hug, but instead, I just took a deep breath and thanked her again. It was hard for me to hold myself to a brisk walk as I left her office and made my way back to the parking lot. Finally, after almost three hours in that office, I was alone in my car. I put my head in my hands and cried hard until I could gather myself long enough to call my mom. I am realizing as I write this how often that happened during this particularly traumatic and emotional phase of my journey.

C.J.
A SEX OFFENDER

I cringed several times during the first day of my court-ordered sex offender group therapy. But maybe my most visceral response was during C.J.'s introduction and brief description of the sex offense that landed him in that dank and drab room with me and about ten other convicted sex offenders. Whenever a new person joined the group, all of the other men in the group needed to present a brief introduction of themselves, including the exact nature of the sex offense they were convicted of and their progress in therapy since that conviction. Everyone's "check-in" had to follow the same format, and Scott was very particular about that. We were routinely scolded like children for leaving something out or listing the important elements of our sex offenses out of order or, worst of all, minimizing what we did or who we hurt in any way.

It was clear during those first introductions that C.J. had been chastised and belittled more than once for not getting it right. For some unknown reason, C.J. volunteered to go first that day, and he delivered his introduction slowly and carefully, sometimes looking up to see how Scott was reacting to it. I could tell he was waiting to be humiliated in front of the group again. I knew he was desperately trying to get it right. C.J. reminded me of an abused puppy who couldn't help peeing on the kitchen floor once in a while.

C.J.'s "check-in" was more than twice as long as anyone else's. It started, like all the others, with a clear description of the offense that he was convicted of. We were overtly instructed not to say "aggravated criminal sexual abuse," or whatever legal terminology was particular to our case. Scott wanted each of us to say, in no uncertain terms, what we actually did. So, instead of saying, "aggravated criminal sexual abuse," C.J. opened with this:

C.J.

"I sexually molested my grandniece. She was three years old. I was sixty-seven."

C.J. was a building inspector for the City of Chicago for almost thirty years when he was offered early retirement. That offer, which came almost a year after his arrest, but before his conviction, kept his sizable pension intact. The taxpayers of Illinois will provide C.J. with quality healthcare and close to $70,000 a year for the rest of his life. This information, along with the fact that C.J. avoided a prison sentence for the offense that he described so matter-of-factly and without any obvious emotion during his check-in, did not go unnoticed by the group. And the rest of the details in C.J.'s check-in only amplified the unpleasant feeling I had in the pit of my stomach that day.

After we described our offenses at the start of our check-in, we were instructed to follow up with three consequences. Most of us listed the legal ramifications of what we did. We listed things like the length of our probation or prison sentence and parole. We always included the fact that we had to register as sex offenders, some of us for ten years and some of us for the rest of our lives. We would usually add the fact that we lost our jobs, our savings, our houses, our cars, etc. A few of us mentioned the impact our offense had on our family members and other loved ones. None of us ever mentioned the mental and emotional consequences of our offenses. C.J. stuck to the legal consequences: four years of sex offender probation, successful completion of sex offender therapy, and lifetime sex offender registration.

The next item on the check-in list was "other acting-out behavior." This is the section that C.J. took the longest to get through. It is also the section that C.J. had to add new behaviors to almost every week. Not only was he continuing to act out while on probation (and he always got caught), C.J. also disclosed more and more of his past behavior as he worked through his therapy. Some of it came up organically with the group, and some of it came up in his individual sessions with Scott. Other behaviors were uncovered as a result of his deception during the polygraph sessions that were mandatory for all of us as part of our therapy.

If we failed the sexual history polygraph, we had two options. We could stick to our guns and take the test again, on our dime this time, or we could come clean about whatever it was that we were refusing to acknowledge. If we chose the latter and it was believable, Scott wouldn't necessarily make us take it again. But C.J. took the polygraph again and again, and new details about his sexual history continued to emerge. The "other acting-out behaviors" that C.J. listed included things such as the prolonged sexual abuse of his niece (the

C.J.

mother of the victim in his case), having sex with women who were passed out or asleep, masturbating while on the job, and providing alcohol to minors in exchange for sex. In what seemed to be an attempt at comic relief, C.J. always added "irresponsible spending" as the last acting out behavior on his list. I let out a spurt of a giggle at this once. It didn't go over well with Scott.

After we were done divulging all of our deviant behavior to the new sex offender in the group, we had to list two contributing factors to our offense and then tell him the most important thing we'd learned in therapy so far. This part usually went pretty quickly because there were clear limits. C.J.'s contributing factors often changed, but he always listed alcoholism and addiction as one of them. This was the first similarity that I noticed in our stories, the first thing that made me see C.J. as more than what he did to his grandniece...and the first thing that helped me find myself in C.J. When he finished his check-in by saying that the most important thing he had learned through his experience in therapy thus far was that his sex offense does not define him, I realized that I desperately needed to listen to the rest of C.J.'s story, and to do my best to learn from it.

BRENT
A SEX OFFENDER

After six months of attending my individual and group therapy sessions for convicted sex offenders, I was no longer one of the new faces in the group. Scott and I had built a respectful working relationship over time, and I was feeling more and more comfortable as an active member of the group. There were times when I found myself actually looking forward to my Tuesday night sessions. It was evident that leaning into the discomfort I felt early on allowed me to grow and learn from this experience in many ways.

Another positive byproduct of surviving the first six months and successfully making my way through the structured levels of the "curriculum" was that I started to feel like I could use what I had learned to help some of the other men in the group. Much like the substance abuse treatment programs I had been participating in, there was a built-in group accountability piece that depended on the group members having more time to mentor some of the newer members who may be struggling through early recovery. Unfortunately, but understandably, the difference with my court-ordered therapy was that it happened to be illegal for convicted sex offenders on probation to have any contact with each other outside of therapy. This meant that any mentoring that happened in my Tuesday night group had to happen in that room and only in that room. If it happened anywhere else, it could result in very real prison time. It wasn't long before I realized that this line was going to be a difficult one for me. On the other hand, it was a good opportunity for me to practice respecting boundaries of all sorts.

Like C.J., Brent was a frequent target of Scott's rage during our group sessions. It was clear that one of the main facets of Scott's philosophy as a seasoned sex offender therapist was the use of public shaming and browbeating as a teaching strategy. He often seemed more like a high school football coach hollering at some linebacker who was caught half-assing a drill at the end of practice than a therapist helping men make important changes to the way they think and act. And although it wasn't effective with me, maybe it did work with some of the other men he counseled. But it didn't seem to work for Brent either.

After receiving one particularly stern and nasty lecture from Scott, Brent approached me outside as I was walking to my car. I was instantly anxious as I felt myself nearing an obvious legal boundary. Brent was beaten and deflated, and he wanted my help. He had recently failed another sexual history polygraph, and he wasn't sure what he needed to do to pass it and move forward with his therapy. He wasn't interested in learning how to beat the system; he genuinely wanted to get better. But he didn't know how. And I was flattered that he apparently considered me to be someone who could help him.

I remember him telling me that he thought I had a good head on my shoulders. The feeling I had when Brent asked me for help that day reminded me, in a way, of how I felt when a struggling student would come to me for guidance or support in the midst of some kind of crisis. It made me feel useful and necessary, like I really was making a difference. I desperately wanted to help Brent clear this mental hurdle so he could continue making progress in therapy. I just didn't know how to do it without crossing or even pushing the moral and legal boundaries involved. I made a quick decision that night to limit my mentoring to a few clear and simple sentences right there in the street in front of Scott's office. I just told him that I wasn't able to learn anything, grow, make changes, or even begin to forgive myself until I faced some pretty ugly truths about my past behavior. I let him know how difficult that was for me and how uncomfortable it made me feel. But I also reminded him that it was completely necessary in order for me to start feeling better and stop making the same mistakes over and over. I advised him to lean into the discomfort of his therapy. It was working for me.

Brent's main therapeutic obstacle was obvious to most of us during his check-in on his first day with the group. When he got to the part of the introduction where he was supposed to describe his sex offense to us using his own words, not the legal terminology of his criminal record, it was painfully clear that he was still in deep denial. The words he chose to describe what he did made us all cringe a little.

He said that he got arrested as a result of a long-term "relationship" he had with his stepdaughter that began when she was thirteen years old. He then launched into a lengthy rationalization of his behavior, minimizing any personal responsibility or negative impact his offense may have had on his victim. The guilt and shame he was feeling were evident to me through his tone and body language, but nothing he was saying could be interpreted as an acknowledgment of any wrongdoing, personal responsibility, or remorse. For several weeks, Brent's go-to response when Scott or any of the rest of us challenged him on his denial and minimization was that his "relationship" with his stepdaughter was due to his wife neglecting both of them. He was sure they wouldn't have been forced into each other's arms if his wife (his victim's mother) had just paid more attention to their emotional and physical needs. He seemed unable or unwilling to look in the mirror and make some difficult but necessary changes.

Brent thanked me for the advice as we stood by my car that night, both of us still on the right side of the line. And as I drove back to my apartment, I remember feeling good about how I handled the situation, and I hoped that my words might help Brent get better. But I also found myself brainstorming other ways I could help him, or maybe even ways I could help some of the other new members of our group. In some convoluted sense, that seemed better and easier than staying on the right path and continuing to look in my own mirror. I was reminded of something one of my counselors in rehab once told me. She said it seemed like I had been more than willing, at certain times in my life, to just light myself on fire in order to keep someone else warm. She was right, and this little brainstorm of mine was a dangerous rabbit hole that I knew I should avoid. And, in the end, I did. But it wasn't easy.

KATHY
A FRIEND'S MOM

Kathy is the mother of one of my best friends in the world, and I have known her for more than thirty years. When I first got out of rehab and was struggling to gather hope and strength to move forward with my life, Kathy was my Mr. Miyagi, and I was her Karate Kid. But instead of painting the fence or waxing the car, Kathy had me weeding the lawn and transplanting lemon verbena...all under the watchful eye of my sensei. And much like Daniel-san with Mr.

Miyagi, it took me more than a few days on the job to realize that everything with Kathy was some kind of life lesson. I wouldn't go on to crane-kick the Cobra Kai at the All Valley Karate Tournament, but I most certainly learned some other valuable skills working in the garden with Kathy. But more than anything else, I will remember how her encouragement, support, and pleasant conversation helped me survive my fight against guilt and shame during the early stages of my sometimes-rocky recovery.

Somehow, helping my friend's mom mow her lawn and weed her garden became one of the most important elements of my therapy and early recovery. My anxiety was palpable the first morning I showed up to help Kathy in her yard. I hadn't seen her or talked to her at all since all of my problems became public knowledge. I had a lot of respect for Kathy, and I felt a special camaraderie with her as a fellow teacher, which probably made her feelings about what I had done a little more complicated. I didn't know what to expect, but Kathy made me instantly comfortable by welcoming me into her kitchen with a warm hug and a hot cup of coffee. We talked for almost an hour before I did any work in the garden that day. Kathy is not known for her filter, but her unbridled honesty and frankness was exactly what I needed back then. Kathy's tough love and compassion were like roundhouse

KATHY

kicks to my heart, just hard enough to get it functioning properly again.

There is some real truth to the theory that many people resemble their pets in one way or another. Well, Kathy doesn't have any pets, but her personality most definitely resembles the beautifully natural and wild landscape that surrounds the house she's lived in for the past thirty-five years. Her gardens are vast and healthy, and she tends to them all with the kind of love and attention that any living thing would be lucky to receive.

The lasting benefits of my semi-regular visits with Kathy cannot be accurately measured here, but I know I will never forget what she did for me at a critical moment in my life. The time I spent digging in Kathy's yard, washing her windows, putting up and taking down her holiday decorations, and chatting about the world with her made me a markedly better man. And she never let me leave without some peppers or garlic from the garden I grew to love almost as much as she did.

MARY BETH
TEACHER, MENTOR, ANOTHER FRIEND'S MOM

When I completed my master's degree in education, I set out to find my first teaching job. Every vein in my body was coursing with enthusiasm and idealism. And I couldn't wait to meet my students, whoever they might be, and to start making a difference. Although I had a deep desire to teach in an underserved neighborhood and help the students who needed it the most, I couldn't resist the urge to apply for a job at my old high school in the suburbs.

Oak Park and River Forest High School (OPRF) is a nationally renowned public school in a community famous for its diversity and open-mindedness. That fact, along with the additional detail that the teachers at OPRF made significantly more money than the national average for public school teachers, meant that English teaching jobs rarely opened up at OPRF. When I realized that there were actually two English openings the year I got my degree, I had to throw my name in the hat. It was a long shot, of course, due to my lack of any real teaching experience. But on top of that, the English Division chairperson at the time happened to be one of my former English teachers, the only one from whom I felt like I had learned anything. But I was in his class during the worst of my years as a self-hating asshole. And I barely managed to get a C in his class.

But despite these two pretty significant red flags, I managed to get through to the final round of interviews that year. But alas, it was not to be. I remember how deflated I felt when my former English teacher called to inform me that the committee had decided to go with someone who had more teaching experience. Looking back, though, it is clear that failing to get that job at OPRF was one of the best things to ever happen to me.

A day or two after I got the bad news about the job at Oak Park, I called Mary Beth in search of some advice and guidance regarding my next step. Mary Beth is a career educator, a former dean at OPRF, and probably my most valuable mentor. She is also my best friend's mom. Mary Beth had made a few phone calls in an attempt to help me secure one of those open positions at OPRF, and I'm sure that had more than a little to do with me making it to the last round of interviews. But now, I was back to square one, and I wasn't exactly looking forward to the job search and application/interview process that I was facing.

Mary Beth wasn't worried, though. She had it all figured out before I even picked up the phone to call her. Through her experience teaching a cohort of graduate students in Chicago, she had some notable connections and influence at Dr. Arlene Acevedo Community Academy (AACA), a high school on the city's northwest side. She spoke highly of the energetic, youthful, and progressive faculty at the school. And she was convinced that not only was this the underserved population that I was thinking of when I decided to become a teacher, it was also a perfect fit for someone with my energy, passion, idealism, and endless naivete. I wouldn't dream of doubting Mary Beth's intuition on such matters. So, on her advice, I just showed up at AACA one day and asked if any English teaching jobs were available. This isn't exactly the usual protocol for applying for a job in the Chicago public school system, but it worked for me. About a month later, I was in my own classroom on the seventh floor, just down the hall from a new history teacher who would end up being my wife and the mother of my children.

That extraordinarily helpful lead on my first teaching job only scratches the surface of the positive impact and influence Mary Beth has had on my life inside and outside of the classroom. In a way, she was standing there next to me throughout my entire career. She was there to encourage me when the seemingly endless and mostly useless bureaucratic obstacles had me losing hope in my ability to make any meaningful difference as a teacher. She was one of the most vocal fans of the spoken word poetry clubs I helped sponsor at both schools where I worked. She attended multiple showcases and fundraising events for the students I worked with. Once, she even invited me to bring a few Spoken Word Club leaders to facilitate a workshop and discussion for her graduate students at DePaul University. And I will never forget seeing her smiling from her seat, front and center, as I addressed my students at a graduation ceremony on the final day of my last year at AACA.

Mary Beth was proud of me and the work I was doing. She made sure to tell me that as often as she could. And I can't tell you how much that meant to me. She is, and always will be, a

MARY BETH

teacher of the highest order. If I was doing good work in Mary Beth's eyes, I knew I was on the right track. That's why she was one of the very first people I thought of when the news of my criminal behavior went public.

I let Mary Beth down, and I was so ashamed. I hated the thought of her coming to believe that maybe she was wrong about me all along, that maybe she shouldn't have helped me secure that first job in Chicago. But I should've known better. I had forgotten about what may be Mary Beth's greatest quality. Much like my dad, Mary Beth knew that everyone had a story, and she collected them and valued them more than any of her possessions. Mary Beth's early teaching career was built through her efforts to help students who had been forgotten or given up on by almost everyone else in the world. She knew the mistakes they made did not define them. So, Mary Beth got to know them, and she helped them. This is the kind of teacher I always tried to be.

When Mary Beth reached out over email to check on me in the early days of what ended up being the bottom of my downward spiral, it gave me that tiny sliver of hope that I needed. If Mary Beth hadn't written me off when she heard the news, maybe some of the other people I loved would one day find similar understanding and forgiveness in their hearts. And since that first reassuring email that I received in my early days of inpatient rehab, Mary Beth has made sure to check in with me and offer kind words and support at least a few times a year. On top of that, Mary Beth wrote a powerful and incredibly kind letter of character reference to the judge presiding over my case. That letter, along with the letters from several other friends, family, former students, and colleagues, are undoubtedly partially responsible for helping the judge come to his eventual decision to spare me from serving any time in prison, essentially saving my life.

But even more than anything else, I will remember the discussions Mary Beth and I have had at various breakfast spots around Chicago over the last few years. When Mary Beth and her husband were in town, we often met up to chat over oatmeal and coffee. And, without fail, at some point during each of those breakfast meetings, I would find myself in tears. The feelings that inspire those tears are complicated, but none of them can be described as sadness. We almost never talked about Mary Beth's son, my best friend, who drew a line in the sand between us when I fled town and checked into rehab back in 2015. She did tell me once that she brought the whole situation up to him a few times early on and that his reaction was less than positive. I didn't doubt that at all. I know her son well, and I'm sure talking to his mom about a situation so complicated and deeply emotional was not something

MARY BETH

that he was all that interested in doing. And I'm sure it only complicated it more knowing that she and I were in contact and that it had been less difficult for her than it had been for him to look past what I had done. And to be honest, it was, and still is, extremely difficult for me to talk about. I knew it made Mary Beth sad, and she knew it made me sad, so we sort of pretended like it wasn't happening. And although it was against my long-standing belief that having those challenging discussions is the best way to heal, learn, and evolve, I think avoiding it in this case was the right thing for both of us to do.

I always made sure to mention at some point during breakfast that I hadn't lost hope that one day her son and I would have the difficult conversation we needed to have, and that we'd cry it out, and that our friendship would eventually resume where it left off. And I still believe that. But in the meantime, maintaining contact with Mary Beth over the past five years has also been a way for me to hold on to my connection with her son. I think that has been an essential factor in how I've coped with his absence in my life. After each of my breakfast pep talks with Mary Beth, we always hugged goodbye before we parted ways. And I always walked to my car feeling rejuvenated and full of hope for my future. Mary Beth's optimism and unmatched positive energy have been a life force for me at the most important times. I don't know where I'd be if I hadn't had Mary Beth on my team for the last thirty years. My heart is overflowing with gratitude as I think about it now.

MAX
A FRIEND AND MARY BETH'S SON

I n the summer of 1991, when I was seventeen years old, my friend Max and I got drunk at my family farm and hatched a plan to travel around the world after we graduated from high school. Our initial plan was to steal my parents' car, drive it to Miami, sell it, and use that money to get a flight to some Caribbean island where we would get jobs and save up what money we would need to circumnavigate the globe. Max would be a scuba instructor, and I would be a bartender, of course. A flawless plan. And I still remain unconvinced that it wouldn't have worked. Sadly, though, nobody will ever know.

When we sobered up sometime the next afternoon, Max and I were drained of our youthful courage, so we started to adjust the time frame and make a few other modifications to our future travel plans. We eventually decided to postpone our adventure until we graduated from college. I'm not sure either of us really believed it would happen, but we spent the next five years talking about it constantly and writing each other letters from our respective college campuses, real letters written on paper and put into envelopes. And when we were back in Oak Park on our breaks, we'd spend countless nights drinking cheap beer in someone's garage or at one of our kitchen tables while we dreamed up new ideas for our big trip. Max always called it "the walk." He must've just read *Walden* or a couple of Robert Frost poems, but I loved it. We even had a big map that we would unfold now and then to help us plot our course. Without much fanfare, we both graduated from college. And we had big plans. But our bank accounts were empty, and I didn't really want to steal my parents' car anymore. So we ended up spending another six months planning "the walk" and painting houses to earn some money before we boarded the first of many flights on our much-anticipated adventure.

MAX

This was one pipe dream that actually came true. Max and I were wearing silly masks of some kind as we boarded a flight to Hawaii on Halloween in 1996. Two other old friends, Butch and Ron, joined us in Australia about a month later, and the four of us would spend the next ten months traveling the world together. The memories and stories we collected on that trip are as dear to me as almost anything else in my life. And to say that our adventure was transformative would be a drastic understatement. Almost twenty-five years have passed since Max and I boarded that first flight, and it is still a relatively common occurrence for me to recall a specific place, person, or moment from that year. And I always get a shiver in my heart as I recognize the perspective I gained through that experience. But one particular moment left a more indelible mark than the rest.

A little over a month into our trip, the four of us left the city limits of Sydney bright and early in a rental car with the steering wheel on the side of the car on which none of us had ever driven from. On top of that, this car had a manual transmission, which may have presented some problems for us even if the stick shift was located on the right side of our seat and operated with the driver's right arm. And, of course, we were instructed to drive on what we considered the wrong side of the road. In the end, I lost the round-robin rock, paper, scissors tournament that we designed to determine who would drive the first shift, which, as I remember, involved traffic and narrow bridges. Although the anxiety and armpit sweat that I felt as I gripped the steering wheel that morning are still fresh in my mind, what weighs heavier is what happened a few hours later.

While we were out drinking and carousing with some locals the night before, we made the snap decision to take a little side trip. That's when we decided to rent a car and head up to the Blue Mountains, a beautiful national park about an hour and a half outside of Sydney. As I remember it, we were going to hike into the park and camp for a night or two. But our plans took a drastic turn shortly after we successfully parked the rental car and left the trailhead.

A couple of hours into our hike, our hangovers were getting the best of us, so we stopped to take in the view from Bridal Veil Falls. It was a beautiful waterfall and climbable rock out-cropping. I sat at the bottom, smoking cigarettes, while the others made their way up for a better view. A few minutes later, I heard one of them scream, "Fuuuuuuuuuuuuuck," and I looked up just in time to see Max's last moment in the air before he landed, headfirst onto a pile of rocks. The noise his skull made as it bounced off of those rocks will never leave me. It was similar to that old-timey knock they used to make when broadcasting baseball games on the radio in the days before the announcers were actually at the games. Butch was close by and immediately rushed to Max's aid. I couldn't see either of them from where I stood, but I heard Butch yell, "Nooooooooooooooo."

The volume and tone of Butch's exclamation sent me scrambling back up the trail in a panicked search for help. I ran as fast as I could, yelling frantically as I searched for the extra adrenaline to continue. It was approaching sunset, and it wasn't common for hikers to spend the night in the park, so the trail was empty, and nobody was responding to my calls for help. Eventually, I ran out of whatever it was that was fueling me, and I fell to my knees and started vomiting and sobbing uncontrollably. I remember thinking about how terrible the phone call to Max's parents was going to be when we'd have to break the news to them that their son was dead, lying in a pile of rocks, thousands of miles away from home. But at exactly that moment, someone from above came to the rescue. Not God. Just some hiker farther up the trail. He yelled down to me asking what the problem was. I told him that we needed help immediately, that one of my friends fell more than twenty feet headfirst onto a pile of rocks, and that he might be dead. The hiker assured me that he'd get help down to us as soon as he possibly could. And I believed him.

As I made my way back down the path toward the spot where I was sure my best friend was lying bloody and lifeless, I was sobbing and struggling to catch my breath. But eventually, I could make out the sight of Butch and Ron kneeling beside Max's body. I remember thinking that it looked a lot like they were praying over him. I started yelling at them, hoping to find out that I was wrong and that Max was okay. But they weren't responding. I thought for sure this was it, that I'd be making that horrible call to Max's parents sometime very soon. But Ron and Butch just couldn't hear me over the sound of the waterfall. When they finally responded, they reported that Max was conscious and breathing. Neither of those things was true when Butch first got to him, but while I was running up the trail, Max had some kind of seizure and came to. He still couldn't really move, and he was definitely confused, but at least he wasn't dead.

After almost an hour, our help from above finally arrived, and Max was airlifted to a hospital in Sydney. The rest of us hiked our way up and out of the Blue Mountains. And then we drove in near silence on the wrong side of the road for a couple more hours, all of us anxious to get to the hospital and find out how bad it was going to be. We were pretty sure that Max had broken his neck or his back. We weren't concerned about the trip we'd been planning and looking forward to for

MAX

so long. We just wanted Max to be alright. And he was, for the most part, depending on who you ask.

When I finally got the chance to call his mom and dad, what I had to report was mostly good news, all things considered. After every test imaginable, it was determined that Max had fractured his skull in two places and that he had a pretty severe concussion. The rest of the damage was only to his muscles. He was sore all over and would have a hard time doing much of anything for a couple of weeks, but the doctors assured him, and the rest of us, that he would be fully functional in a month's time. As it turns out, Max found his rock bottom about twenty years before I did, but "the walk" would go on, almost exactly as Max and I had planned it.

All these years later, I can still feel the fear, sadness, and panic I felt as it all unfolded. But I can also feel the pure joy and relief that I experienced when I learned that Max was alive and that there would be no real or lasting damage from his fall. That day, I think I felt what it was like to lose my best friend... but a short while later, the nightmare was over, and I had him back. That is what I am hoping to feel again someday very soon.

I only spoke with Max three or four times in the first five or so years after I disappeared in a puff of smoke and checked into rehab. I remember talking to him on the phone very briefly from a Starbucks near my brother's house as we were getting ready for our trip to get me some much-needed help in Minnesota. It was a comfort to hear his voice in the middle of the storm I was in. And he made sure to let me know that he would be there for me when I returned. He asked what he could do to help. I could tell Max was worried about me, and I hated that I was making him feel bad in any way. I tried to assure him that day that I would make it through this, that I was headed to one of the best drug rehabilitation facilities in the world. And I apologized for letting him down. I know that I let him down and that it hasn't been easy for him.

Five weeks after that conversation from Starbucks, as I approached my release date from rehab in Minnesota, I sent an email reaching out to all of my friends to let them know that I was coming home soon. But I also needed more help. While I was off in the Northwoods trying to figure out what went wrong and how to fix it, my wife was taking care of our kids, going to work, and trying to keep her head above water in the ruins I left her to deal with. And during that time, she came to the understandable conclusion that I should probably find somewhere else to live when I returned from rehab. It crushed me when she let me know I wouldn't be coming back to our home, but it was definitely what was best for her and our family. And I know that it couldn't have been easy for her to make that decision or break that difficult news to me.

MAX

But when I sent my friends that email asking them to help me find a place to stay, they mobilized quickly and came up with a number of potential solutions. Max responded almost immediately. He made sure to tell me that I was welcome to stay at his house with his family. He also offered to get me an apartment if I thought that would be better. But sometime over the next few days, everything changed. I'm still not sure why, but I'm guessing it was a delayed response to the way I had deceived and betrayed him in the years leading up to that moment.

Luckily, my sister came to my rescue and graciously offered to let me move in with her and her roommate on the North Side of Chicago. I didn't need to take Max up on his offer for indefinite housing, but he did say he'd give me a ride to my sister's apartment when I landed back in the real world. But the day before I was set to fly back to Chicago, Max sent me a short and kind of cold email saying that he wouldn't be able to pick me up after all.

Over the next couple of years, Max and I exchanged dozens of texts. At one point, it got pretty heated and dangerously confrontational. And at the end of one of these infrequent and unproductive text exchanges, he sent me this message: "You abused a vulnerable, young girl. It's disturbing, disgusting, and unforgivable." I don't need to look at my phone and scroll back to remember his exact wording. That sentence is burned into my conscience. And the way he felt when he wrote it was real and can't be denied. And it just kills me that I made him feel that way. I don't blame him, and I know that he's not alone.

I have a strong suspicion that Max's initial reluctance to respond positively to my attempts to make amends and rebuild our friendship has a more complex origin and foundation than it may seem on the surface. I believe that I know him better than anyone outside of his family. And I can say with confidence that he knows me well, maybe even better than my mom...or anyone else for that matter. That's why I'm positive it has to be more nuanced and complicated than just the simple refusal to look past what I did on those four occasions during those three weeks of my life. And that is why I refuse to give up hope that Max and I will indeed patch things up and rebuild our friendship someday down the road. It might not happen this week or this year, but I truly believe that it will happen. I have never been able to accept the idea that the friendship that I value so much is just over and done with, that our relationship going forward will continue to be a collection of polite nods and superficial pleasantries. Both of us would hate that. I'm sure of it.

MAX

My trip around the world came to an unplanned and premature ending a couple of months before Max, Butch, and Ron boarded their flight back to Chicago, mostly because I ran out of money and excuses somewhere in the middle of Europe. As it turns out, I missed the chance to wrap up our year abroad with a summer in western Europe due to five or six uneventful and ill-advised side trips to various gambling establishments and other houses of ill-repute in Cairo, Prague, Mombasa, and Vienna. And I'm probably forgetting a few other cities.

Once all four of us were back where we came from, our lives split off in different directions, but the bond I share with those guys is strong and enduring. Unfortunately for me, though, while I was off seeing the world and preparing myself for the next stage of my life, my parents were readying themselves for a transition in their own lives.

About six months after Max and I boarded that first flight, my mom and dad had the gumption to sell the house that they'd owned for almost twenty-five years, the only house I had ever lived in. My dad finally hung up his bowties and retired from the job he only kind of enjoyed, and they moved up to our family farm, the very location where Max and I first dreamt up our idea to travel the world together. Their parenting duties were all but done, so they thought, and my mom and dad were ready to start the best stage of their life together. This meant that I was left with almost no choice when I came back and noticed a different family living in my childhood home. So I put my tail between my legs and moved in with my brother and his future wife near Wrigley Field (they didn't have much of a choice either), and I started pursuing my dream to become an English teacher in some inner-city school where they would need me the most.

Two and a half years later, I'd have a master's degree in education, and I'd be writing lesson plans for my first classes at Dr. Arlene Acevedo Community Academy in Chicago's Humboldt Park neighborhood. Max would end up in Washington, DC, well on his way to becoming a lawyer. Butch would be trading options in Chicago, and Ron would be slinging industrial real estate in Arizona. But the four of us never lost touch. Max and I always kept up with each other, checking in frequently to discuss our progress or to rehash some of the more noteworthy moments from "the walk." Max was always so supportive and encouraging about my decision to be a teacher, and I was consistently impressed and inspired by his drive and passion for becoming a lawyer. I think part of me wanted to do what he was doing, and part of him wanted to do what I was doing.

Eventually, we both moved on from a job or two, and Max was back in Chicago after brief stints in New York and Paris. He was working in the financial industry in some capacity that I could never quite understand. It was over my head for sure. But there was no doubt that he was successful. I had moved on from my classroom in Chicago to accept a job teaching English at our old high school in Oak Park, five years after my former English teacher informed me that they were going with someone who had more teaching experience. And although I arrived with some very valuable experience under my belt, I never felt as traditionally qualified as the other teachers in the building. But I knew I would be a good fit at my old school and that I would make a difference in the lives of the students I would be lucky enough to teach. I was riding high after my five years of teaching "at-risk" students at AACA, and I think that confidence must've been part of the reason that the interview committee and the administration at OPRF decided to take a chance on someone like me. I often wonder how they feel about that decision today. I hope it's not all regret.

In my ten years working at OPRF, I came into my own as a teacher, coach, and mentor. And I remain proud of the way I went about doing my job. And although this is something notoriously hard for teachers to measure, I feel good about the results of my work. I did my best to have a positive impact on the student population that needed the most help, but I didn't ignore the students who were lucky enough to find themselves, like me, on the right side of privilege. In my tenure at OPRF, I taught all three academic tracks and all four grade levels. I coached boys' and girls' tennis for six years, and I was one of the proud sponsors of OPRF's nationally renowned Spoken Word Club. And Max loved hearing all about it. He came to almost all of the Spoken Word Club performances and competitions, usually sitting right next to his mom. And he almost always cried. We all considered him our superfan. And I could tell that, like his mom, he was proud of the work I was doing.

While I was at OPRF, I would sometimes get positive letters or emails from students or parents, and I always shared them with Max. He and my mom were the only people I felt comfortable patting myself on the back in front of. And shortly before things went sideways, I forwarded an email to him that I received from the student involved in my case. In her email, she thanked me for taking the time to listen to her story and help her through a very difficult crisis. She went on to say that I saved her life. It was the kind of letter that I lived for, one full of reassurance that I was indeed a good man, that I was making a difference in the best possible way. But this was before I crossed any professional, moral, or legal boundaries with the student who wrote the letter. Within weeks of receiving that email, everything would change.

MAX

Max and I still run into each other at holiday parties and our book club meetings. And we always greet each other warmly and spend a few minutes talking about our kids before we start mumbling about the weather or something else that neither of us really cares about. I can always sense the tension between us, and I'm guessing Max also feels uncomfortable with all that we *aren't* saying. It does get easier and easier each time we see each other, though, and that is what fuels my hope that one day we will sit down and get it all on the table. We will cry. Then we will laugh. Then I will have my friend back again. This time, I'll be the one recovering from a nearly fatal fall.

BOOK CLUB

At the peak of the selfish immaturity of my adolescence, I found myself surrounded by a group of friends at some party in someone's basement. I remember being interrogated by a few of them who seemed especially angry about my relationship with one of their girlfriends, or cousins, or sisters. I honestly don't remember the details of the discussion, but I'm sure I was guilty in some way for at least some of what they were accusing me of. I was no angel back then. And I didn't feel good about the person I was becoming. But this confrontation, this very specific moment in time, still causes a visceral response when I'm reminded of it.

After shouting a few questions and accusations at me, one of my friends threw me to the ground, and another started kicking me. I just curled myself into a ball and tried to cover my head. I remember looking up long enough to see three of the guys looking down at me, the three guys whom I'd known for the longest, the three guys whom I considered brothers, but they *weren't* kicking me. They were just standing there, hands at their sides, mouths shut, with maybe a sliver of shame in their eyes. I don't know how long I was on the ground before the kicking stopped, but I do recall hesitantly and carefully picking myself up and pushing my way past them. I desperately needed to get up the stairs and out of that house. I know for a fact that I didn't say a word to any of them. Although I did spend several years coming up with all of the things I wish I had said. But, in the end, maybe my slow and silent walk-off sent the perfect message to my old friends. And maybe if I had stopped to give them a piece of my mind, the beating I received would've gotten worse, or more likely, I would've just started crying. And that wouldn't have been a good look at all.

I remember being incredibly sad and confused for a few days after the incident in the basement that night. And I also remember feeling empty and suddenly without purpose.

BOOK CLUB

And somehow, I was full of guilt and shame. Those feelings remain familiar to me today. As cliche as it sounds, the very public rebuking I received at that party felt like the end of the world to me. And with three semesters left in high school, I suddenly didn't have a single close friend. But as devastating as that felt, I managed to scrounge up just enough dignity to stop myself from crawling back to my former friends who had very recently either physically assaulted me or just stood there, stone-faced, watching the assault.

After a week or two of what felt like a zombie-walk through classes, tennis practice, and anything else I was supposed to be doing, something amazing happened. I don't recall who it was, but I'd like to think it was Max, who at tennis practice one day just started treating me as his friend as if I'd always been his friend. Slowly, others followed his lead. And within a few weeks, I was welcomed into an entirely new group of friends. All of them I had known in some way or another through school or sports. One of them I had known since kindergarten. But most of these guys had been on the wrong side of the shitty personality I had developed over the previous year or two. But, to this day, none of them has ever mentioned that to me.

Looking back now, I realize that Max and the others must've remembered the way I was before I turned into the kind of person it's so easy to hate. And something in them must've known that it wasn't too late for me to turn back and become someone I wasn't embarrassed to be. And there is no doubt that their friendship was exactly what I needed at that time of my life, and I won't forget how easy they made it for me to bounce back.

Over the next several years, this new friend group helped me find a new path and purpose. I began to evolve and become a better human being. And regardless of where our lives have led us, I will always consider them my brothers. Many of us have moved back to our old neighborhood. And the friendships we built so long ago remain as strong as they ever were. We've traveled the world together, stood up at each other's weddings, and supported each other through other important transitions in life. We've celebrated our career accomplishments together, and we've mourned and grieved the loss of loved ones together. And we continue to raise our kids together. But the most impressive and significant evidence of our enduring friendship is our book club. Yes, you read that right. For the last seven years or so, we have been getting together about once a month to talk to each other about books, of all things. And, contrary to what everyone who has ever known us might think, we take it pretty seriously, at least for the first hour or two.

BOOK CLUB

There was a time when I would have laughed at the thought of us starting some kind of book club. It didn't seem to be the direction any of us were headed. For many years, we spent most of our time together drinking copious amounts of cheap beer and having superficial discussions about sports, girls, and maybe music. But, given time, we all grew up. And we turned out to be a collection of pretty extraordinary men, each one of us with a story of our own. And although there are still occasions when our get-togethers may look and sound a little bit like they did when we were teenagers, we *do* have a book club. And that has to say something about us.

We take turns choosing important and meaningful books to over-analyze, review, and discuss on a regular basis. We even sweat over our menu selections when it's our turn to host, wondering if the meal and specialty cocktails we decided on will accurately reflect the themes of that month's book selection. And on the night our book club meets, we always greet each other with warm man-hugs and a smattering of inappropriate jokes before we sit down to eat. Once our thematically appropriate dinner concludes, we get right to business and begin what is usually an insightful discussion about literature and the world. And it's amazing every time. I am not ashamed to admit that our monthly book club meetings may be the one thing I look forward to more than anything else these days. But it hasn't always been that way.

When I learned of my friend's brilliant idea to create and organize a regular book club consisting of all of my closest friends, I couldn't have been more excited. I loved it when there was an occasion for the whole crew to come together. But as we all got older and started our families and careers, occasions like those became increasingly rare. And they usually involved the birthday of a small child, which is great for the small child, but not that conducive to the type of fun we usually liked to have together. This book club idea was bound to give us new life…every month. On top of that, I was an English teacher at the time. And talking about books just happened to be one of my favorite things to do. So I threw myself headfirst into the book club for the first year or two of its existence. But it wouldn't be long before my addiction started gathering steam, and things began to change.

At first, I started showing up to book club late and drunk, usually with a small baggie of cocaine in one of my socks. I'd sneak off to the bathroom for a few bumps every half hour or so, and then I'd start talking even faster than my usual pace. Sometimes, I never stopped talking. And I'm sure my rude interruptions became more annoying as they increased in frequency. There is no doubt that I eventually stopped listening

BOOK CLUB

to what anyone else had to say. And I almost always woke up feeling terrible the next morning.

And that terrible feeling is what eventually led to my book club attendance becoming sporadic at best. Every time I bailed, though, the embarrassment and guilt I felt got worse. And as those negative feelings fueled my addiction, the possibility of me showing up at book club decreased exponentially. The guilt and shame continued to gain momentum, and predictably, I continued to double down on my drinking and drug use. See how that works? It's a pattern of behavior familiar to most addicts and alcoholics. As we slowly abandon more activities and people we love the most, it only gets worse for us. At some point, our race to the bottom begins, and although we manage to get it together for brief periods of time, we eventually realize that we will never be able to put an end to this downward spiral with sheer willpower or determination alone. Unfortunately, it often takes years for us to accept this sad truth and ask for the help we need.

After a couple of years of behavior like that, I stopped coming to book club meetings altogether. And when I found my rock bottom and shipped out to rehab, I received dozens of emails from the guys I had betrayed and abandoned while I was losing control of my life. Without exception, their emails were full of the kind of love and support that my old friends had been giving me for years. I wasn't surprised by that, but I certainly didn't feel worthy of their compassion and encouragement at the time.

As I eventually progressed and stumbled my way through early recovery, I started showing up to our book club again. It was difficult and awkward at first, and I was filled with anxiety and emotion each and every time I found the strength to attend. But there were still months when I just couldn't do it. I desperately wanted everything to be normal again, but rushing it wasn't an option. It took a couple of years of sporadic attendance, but it finally started to feel normal again. In fact, I haven't missed a book club meeting in almost a year now. I don't stay as late as I used to, for obvious reasons, but I'm always one of the first ones there. And I'm never drunk (sometimes one of the guys will even make me a mock cocktail). And I don't sneak off to the bathroom to snort cocaine anymore. But I probably still talk too much. As it turns out, all of the therapy and rehab in the world won't change a tiger's stripes. Most importantly, though, I wake up the morning after book club feeling hopeful and inspired, without even the slightest hint of guilt or shame. And I don't get the hangovers either.

DANA
MY EX-WIFE

I wish I could say that my marriage was already in trouble before my addiction really took off, or that maybe Dana and I weren't good for each other anyway, or that our eventual divorce was inevitable and all for the best. But life is rarely that cut and dried, that black and white, that simple, or that easy to swallow. The truth is, Dana and I loved each other. We had a great life together, and things were just getting better and better for a long time. We were so lucky. But a combination of factors out of our control, along with several bad decisions and mistakes on my part, put an end to the plans we had for our family. The future both of us imagined didn't die all of a sudden on the day I got suspended from my job or on the day I got arrested and charged with the crimes I committed. The process started a few years earlier, and I didn't stop it. That is something that I will have to live with forever.

Dana and I met at Dr. Arlene Acevedo Community Academy. I was fresh out of graduate school, and it was my first teaching job. I couldn't have been more excited about being there. Dana was beginning her second year of teaching, but it was her first year at AACA. She had recently relocated to Chicago on a whim after teaching high school history for one year in Michigan. We were assigned to teach the same group of about one hundred students in our first year at AACA. I would be their English teacher and Dana would be their World History teacher. And we clicked almost immediately.

Dana was, and still is, the perfect blend of hippie and intellectual. And she was beautiful without the appearance that she was trying to impress anyone. She often taught her classes barefoot (not anymore, I don't think), and I noticed right away that she laughed at my jokes with more passion and regularity than any of my other colleagues. Needless to say, I had a good feeling about Dana right from the start.

DANA

After my mom and dad came to visit me at AACA that fall, mostly just to see with their own eyes that I really was a teacher, my dad took me aside and told me that I should "make a move" on that cute history teacher who wasn't wearing any shoes. It took about seven months, but I did eventually "make a move" on Dana. And, against all odds, it worked. From that point forward, our relationship proceeded at a fairly rapid pace.

A few months later, when the school year came to an end, Dana and I embarked on a month-long road trip, crisscrossing the country in my old Saab. And spending twenty-four hours a day together, sharing one small tent every night for a month, solidified everything I was hoping for. When we returned to school for our second year at AACA in the fall, I knew in my heart that it was only a matter of time before we would be married.

A few years later, one of our favorite students from the group we taught in our first year helped me propose to Dana in her classroom after school. And the three of us cried together when Dana said yes. But we had to cut the celebration short so Dana wouldn't be late to her National Organization for Women meeting. We both laughed and cringed at how the group might receive it if she called in to say that she had to miss that night's meeting because a man had just proposed to her. How very un-feminist that would be, we thought. I remember sitting alone in our apartment, full of anxiety and anticipation, waiting for her to return from that meeting. I was ordered not to break the news of our engagement to anyone until we could do it together. And when that time finally came, we called our families first. Everyone was happy for us. And without exception, they were excited but unsurprised by our news. I do remember, though, that both of our dads were especially pleased. And that meant a lot to us.

As soon as I got to know Dana, it was clear that her dad was her guiding light. She admired him in countless ways, and aside from his right-leaning political convictions, Dana wanted nothing more than to be just like him. He was compassionate, caring, loyal, hard-working, responsible, and witty…a great man by anyone's standards. And Dana's dad was her hero, much like my dad was mine. But sadly, about a year before my dad got sick, Dana lost her hero to an aggressive and unrelenting cancer that slowly poisoned most of his internal organs and ended his life in a truly awful way. The loss of her father will be with Dana forever, but the positive impact he made on her while he was alive will remain, as well.

In a way, as sad as it was that both of us were forced to face such a difficult time in our lives without the guidance and support of our fathers, there was something to be grateful for too. Both of our heroes died while our relatively new

DANA

family was healthy and thriving. It was apparent to all who knew us back then that we had found true love and genuine happiness in our lives. There were no warning signs of the storm that was forming beneath the surface. Whatever our dads were thinking and feeling as they faced their inevitable deaths, they weren't worried about us or our family. Their painfully premature deaths spared them the anxiety, disappointment, and sadness that the rest of our family and loved ones were forced to deal with on account of my actions. On the other hand, their continued presence in our lives would have made everything easier for *us*. I have thought of both of our dads often as Dana and I have struggled to save our family and preserve the undeniable legacy of our fathers.

Dana does extensive research before even the most seemingly insignificant purchase. She learned this practical and financially responsible practice from her dad, who was known to consult Consumer Reports and at least one other source before making his final decision on a new toaster or coffee maker. On the other hand, as I learned from observing my dad's spending habits over the years, I bought almost everything without much thought at all. In fact, on the rare occasion that I buy clothes for myself, even today, I rarely take the time to try anything on. If I get home and discover that something I bought during the thirty minutes or less that I spent in the store doesn't fit, I just put it in a bag with the tags still on to be donated at a later date, or, more likely, to just hang, unworn, at the back of my closet with several other too-small shirts and too-tight pants. This glaring difference in our shopping styles turns out to be a perfectly symbolic representation of the two distinct personalities that Dana and I have developed over time. To someone who didn't know us, it may seem like this should've been some sort of red flag, but I think it was part of what made us such a good match…in the old "yin to my yang" kind of way.

There is no doubt that Dana helped me evolve into a more thoughtful, responsible, and careful human being than I was before I met her. Although it's obvious that I still have a ways to go. But I would also contend that Dana probably benefited from my sometimes impulsive, go-with-the-flow, don't-worry-about-it approach to life. I have always admired and envied the practical, responsible, and thoughtful side of Dana, and I certainly needed some of that in my life. And I'd like to believe that Dana found something to admire and envy about the silly, irrational, adventurous, and irresponsible side of my winning personality. Either way, I think it's fair to say that in the almost fifteen years that Dana and I spent together, we each made significant progress toward that stretch of middle ground between us. And I think both of us are better for it. I know I am.

DANA

Dana once told me, several months after I left the house and headed for the safety of an inpatient rehab facility in the woods, that she thought her love for me died on impact the day I told her the truth about the secret life I had been living. I'll never forget that analogy, and I have thought of it often over the last six years...mostly because I know that it's true. Looking back and imagining how things could've been had my dad not gotten sick, had I asked for help as soon as I knew things were spiraling out of control, or had I not chaperoned that school trip to Ireland doesn't do anyone any good.

But that didn't stop me from almost constantly ruminating over it for the first couple of years after the proverbial shit hit the fan. It fit perfectly into my lifelong pattern of making bad decisions, damaging relationships, hurting people, and then never forgiving myself for it. But that is the kind of thinking that has fed my addictions for years. I needed to find a way to snap out of that cycle if there was ever going to be hope for me to live a happy and healthy life again. I did everything I could to reset my attention onto the moment I was living. And, somehow, it finally started to work. It took time, and it still isn't natural for me to think like this, but it has made all the difference.

I will continue to process the events of my past and, whenever possible, make amends for the damage I've done, but the best thing I can do today is to take all the steps necessary to prevent myself from repeating the same mistakes I've been making since I was a teenager. I am not sure how much better my life will get if I keep doing the next right thing, but I do know how much worse it will get if I don't continue to make my recovery a priority for the rest of my life. One of the most repeated sayings in twelve-step meetings and rehab facilities is, "If nothing changes, nothing changes." It's so simple but so inarguably true.

JASPER AND ROCKET
MY KIDS

Although scientists haven't yet discovered a gene specifically responsible for the disease of addiction, there is no doubt that it runs in families, and mine is no exception. Luckily for my kids, though, their mom's side of the family is free of the disease that was passed down on my side, like my grandpa's old underwear or something else nobody really wants. To be fair, my mom's genetic line only shows faint signs of addiction, just enough to make

Christmas interesting. On the other hand, my dad's family has been passing grandpa's dirty underwear around for generations. Not everyone has to wear them, of course, but if you threw a handful of nickels into our family tree, you'd be sure to hit more than one of us who has at least tried them on a few times. But if there is anything humanly possible that I can do to keep that dirty underwear away from our two kids, I will go to the end of the Earth to do it. A lot of Jasper and Rocket's risk for inheriting the disease can be addressed and eliminated with some appropriate preventative measures, like awareness and education. But I plan on using some good old-fashioned fear tactics too.

One of the benefits of being the offspring of a father who is a drug addict and a mother who was married to a drug addict for almost ten years is that it will be nearly impossible for any of the early warning signs of addiction to go unnoticed by one or both of your parents. Sadly, the research shows that the two kids Dana and I brought into this world have an increased likelihood of having some kind of unhealthy addiction at some point in their lives. But I can't imagine a world where we wouldn't diagnose and seek treatment for said addiction at the earliest possible stage. In fact, Dana and I are quite likely to *mis*diagnose our kids as addicts more than once before either of them turns sixteen. Better safe than sorry, I suppose. On the other hand, I anticipate some fairly spirited pushback against our probable over-analysis of Jasper and Rocket's behavior as they stumble, stagger, and eventually survive their teenage years. But I'm confident that Dana and I will be ready for whatever they throw at us.

In addition to our involuntary exposure to the dangerous pitfalls of addiction, Dana and I both have years of experience teaching high school students. And although Dana was always more of a rule follower during her adolescence than I was during mine, both of us also learned a thing or two while we were still young. Our personal and professional resumes indicate that we qualify as experts on the sometimes-devastating consequences of addiction *and* adolescence. But there are no guarantees that Dana and I will be successful in our mission to guide Jasper and Rocket through a trauma-free, misery-free, and disaster-free adolescence. I have met more than one child born to two therapists, for example, who turned out to be less than psychologically balanced. And I've read enough books and heard enough songs to know that the son of a preacher-man doesn't always end up on the right side of all ten commandments.

All of that being said, I believe that the two parents Jasper and Rocket drew from the unfairly stacked deck of caregivers will give them better-than-average odds of ending up with a full house, or at least a high straight. The two most important cards in their hands will always do everything in their power to make sure they grow up to live healthy, happy, and rewarding lives. And if I were a betting man (I am), I'd be all-in on our two boys. But, as it turns out, I probably shouldn't bet on anything anymore. Either way, you know what I mean. It's a sure thing. But that doesn't mean I won't worry about it.

Our oldest son, Jasper, has inherited some of what I consider to be good about me. But he has also been blessed with all of the best parts of Dana's personality. He is kind, responsible, creative, thoughtful, open-minded, curious, intelligent, and genuine. And he's so damn cute. But some of our other not as desirable traits may have slipped past the goalie too. Like me, Jasper is so, so, so, so, so sensitive. This is a blessing and a curse that I have lived with for as long as I can remember. Yet, despite being problematic for me at many stages of my life, I wouldn't trade it in for anything. It's something I still deal with on an almost daily basis. One of the devil's many well-versed advocates might even say that this kind of over-sensitivity could serve as the genesis of a problem for someone who is genetically predisposed to addiction. I have to admit that I have met plenty of people like me and Jasper in AA meetings and rehab. Just another thing Dana and I have to keep an eye on as we help him understand and navigate the world around him.

JASPER AND ROCKET

It would not be absurd to say that, since he was approximately ten years old, Jasper has been more reasonable and responsible than I will ever be. There is no need to debate the origins of this particularly beneficial character trait that Jasper undoubtedly possesses. It is at least 100 percent Dana. We didn't know he would turn out this way when we decided to give him Dana's last name, but it most definitely fits. This was clear when Jasper was maybe four years old, and he spent an entire day with Dana's dad, designing and building a live trap for some pesky squirrel who had been causing trouble at Dana's family lake house up north.

Almost ten years later now, and there is still so much of Dana's dad in Jasper's personality and general demeanor. Like his grandpa and his mom, Jasper is likely to spend a week or two doing the appropriate research before making almost any purchase, whether it be a part for a computer that he's planning to build or the scooter most suitable for doing tricks and jumps. And, unlike his dad or his dad's dad, for that matter, Jasper won't just assume that the most expensive one is the best one and the one he must have. Like his mom and his mom's dad, Jasper will be sure to find the best deal. "It was a steal," he'll tell anyone who asks him about it.

I've always been envious of the artistic talents of my aunt Coco, my cousin Jesse, my dad, and my brother. And I added

Jasper to that list almost immediately following his first crayon-on-napkin masterpiece. There is definitely some kind of visual art/creativity gene on my dad's side of the family. Aunt Coco found a way to make a career out of it, and I feel like my cousin, dad, or brother could have done the same if they had chosen that path in life. Jasper most definitely fits in that lucky subgroup of my family. He won an award in elementary school for a pencil drawing of some African landscape that he could've only visited in his imagination. Unless, of course, he managed to sneak away for a quick trip when I wasn't paying attention, I am pretty sure Jasper hadn't yet witnessed the vast plains of the Serengeti. His art teacher made him erase the live-action poop he drew behind one of the elephants, but he was like eight years old. What did she expect? Jasper's artwork serves as wallpaper throughout most of my apartment. And I often find myself admiring it and wonder-hoping if he will choose a career path someday that will allow him to put his innate creativity to use. Either way, Jasper has so much to give in so many ways, and I can't wait to see where he goes and what he does.

Rocket reminds me of me in all of the best ways. He's witty, sensitive, and charismatic. He loves the spotlight, but he's also kind of shy and insecure. He's incredibly in tune with the emotions and feelings of other people and seems to have some innate desire to take care of them. And he's so damn cute. But there is no denying some of the red flags that are beginning to poke through the dirt around him. Screen addiction is no longer just some light-hearted phrase that parents use when talking about how much their kids love video games. It's real, and it can be devastating in many of the same ways substance abuse is devastating. And our struggle with Rocket and his screen use may be the product of what many consider developmentally normal behavior for a kid his age, but it sure seems to me like it's a little harder for him to turn off the gaming console than it is for the other kids.

It is often said that what separates the "normies" from us addicts is the fact that, when we start using our drug of choice, we don't have an off switch. Rocket's reaction to dying batteries in his gaming controller or his iPad makes me think that he might have a faulty or damaged off switch, at the very least. And the feeling he gets before, during, and after playing video games is also quite familiar to me. And it makes me sad to see Rocket experience those negative feelings, especially at such a young age, when he doesn't have the emotional or intellectual maturity to process those feelings or even begin to put them into words. There are days when I feel like a future battle with addiction is inevitable for Rocket, and the guilt I experience around that feeling isn't pleasant. But it will also fuel my vigilance as I try to be the best kind of dad for both of my boys…to nurture them, protect them, listen to them, support them, guide them, and love them unconditionally and without reservation.

On the other hand, since second or third grade, Rocket has been doing something that always warms my heart. It has occasionally even brought me to tears. Upon meeting a new person or getting to spend some extra time with someone he is already familiar with, Rocket always finds the time to ask them about their lives, and he almost always tries to learn as much as he can about each person's story. This is an especially rare character trait for a kid who still has a couple more years to serve in elementary school. And it can certainly be a bit disarming to the unsuspecting adult who finds themself on the other side of one of these interviews.

These are a few of the tried-and-true questions Rocket uses to get the conversation started: "What is your dream day? If you could have dinner with anyone in the world, who would it be? What do you think happens when you die? Did you grow up with anyone who ended up becoming famous?" (I suspect this question comes from the fact that Rocket thinks it's pretty cool that my dad briefly lived in the same neighborhood as a very young Bob Dylan.) "Do you think everyone has problems?" That's my favorite one. And Rocket always remembers how people answer his probing questions. It's clear that he is already collecting stories. And that makes me happy.

I can't help but think of my dad when I notice Rocket embarking on another one of his missions to get to know someone. Some of the fondest memories I have of my dad from my adulthood take place at the long, barnwood table at our family farm in Wisconsin. He spent more nights than I can count sitting at the head of that table, generously pouring wine for whomever was willing to stay up and talk with him. And in the last ten or twenty years of his life, I can barely remember my dad spending more than a few minutes talking about himself. He was especially interested in everyone else's job (I suspect this was due in large part to the fact that he didn't exactly love the job he did for thirty years). But his questions never stopped at the surface. My dad made sure to ask people about their dreams, sometimes about why they *weren't* pursuing them. After my dad died, more than one of my friends told me that they will be forever grateful for the sometimes subtle, but often not so subtle, nudges he gave them regarding some big life decision they ended up making or not making. As it turns out, my dad was some kind of modern-day Yoda, albeit with a better haircut and expensive shoes.

My biggest fear, which was born shortly after the doctors discovered the tumor in my dad's brain, and eventually gave my already blossoming addiction just the push it needed for it to spiral out of control, has always been that I had done, was currently doing, or would someday do something that would cause any kind of emotional, mental, or physical harm to either of my beautifully perfect boys. And the sad truth is that some of my actions during the early and important years of their childhood will have a lasting impact on their lives. There were obstacles in their development that wouldn't have existed if I hadn't done what I had done...if I hadn't crossed so many lines and put all of our lives in danger. These obstacles will continue to cause aftershocks for both of them, and my past behavior will undoubtedly create unnecessary hardship at different stages of their lives. Both boys will someday have difficult feelings to process as they learn, mature, and evolve. And I will always feel responsible for that. But, I am also aware, from a vantage point safely removed from the eye of the storm, that my sons have gained something positive through this experience, as well.

Because of all of this, Jasper and Rocket will be more resilient, more empathetic, and more compassionate human beings. Some of these early life experiences will have given them a perspective on the world they otherwise wouldn't have had. Who knows, maybe it will be part of what will one day draw one or both of them to a career in social services.

Maybe one or both of them will turn out to be an amazing social worker, a therapist, an activist, a politician…or even a teacher. And like everyone else, I suppose, Jasper and Rocket will have personalities composed of, in some unknown proportion, a perfect combination of the nature they were born with and the nurturing they received. And when I consider their parents, their parents' parents, and all of the other love that surrounds them, I can't help but believe that both of them will grow up to be the best kind of men. And I will always be proud to be their dad.

27

MY MOM

"Think before you act." My mom gave me this sound advice at least once a day for most of my teenage years, and come to think of it, she continued that practice well into my twenties. And it's not out of the ordinary for her to spring it on me once in a while, even today. She has always known that this has been my greatest weakness. My impulsivity and disabling desire for instant gratification have been creating problems in my life for as long as I can remember. I've always been a risk taker, and I usually got away with it until very recently. And that only fueled my overconfidence in the decisions I made. But, eventually, my luck was bound to run out. I have joked about this over the years, but I think I can trace this problem back to a conversation I had with my best friend, Billy Brachman, in third grade.

Billy and I had been out riding our bikes in the rain and mud one spring afternoon, and somehow we lost track of time. It became clear that I wasn't going to make it home for dinner as I had promised my mom. I stopped pedaling long enough to tell Billy that I better head back home, and I expressed to him some of my anxiety about the trouble I was going to be in when I walked through the front door of my house, tired, muddy, and over an hour late. Well, my best friend looked me dead in the eye, and he calmly said to me, "You won't get in trouble until you go home." He went on to put together a pretty convincing case that I should keep splashing through puddles on my dirt bike and just deal with my mom and dad whenever I decided I was ready to call it a day. I have referred to this as the Billy Brachman rule ever since, and I have used it often.

At some point during my time in college, I gave this dangerous life philosophy of mine a new name. I started calling it "Jayism." I told anyone who would listen that this ridiculous personal religion had only two tenets: 1. If it feels good, do it. 2. If it starts to hurt, stop doing it. Turns out, I had an

MY MOM

unfortunate inability to stick to the second tenet. And that continued to cause problems for me and the people around me for years. I'd like to take this opportunity to publicly declare Jayism and the Billy Brachman rule grossly ineffective, harmful, and frankly, in my experience, counterproductive.

I'm not going to lie, choosing to follow Billy Brachman's lead instead of heeding my mom's advice, along with my penchant for treating the consequences of my actions as nothing more than an afterthought, resulted in some worthwhile and valuable adventures in my early life. If I had flown by the seat of my pants less often when I was a younger man, I most definitely would have missed out on some experiences that I wouldn't trade for anything. But, all of that considered, it is abundantly clear that I should've taken my mom's incessant yet sage advice a little more seriously.

I don't think I even considered what the words of my mom's advice actually meant or internalized the lesson she had been trying so desperately to teach me until *not thinking* landed me in jail and *not thinking* caused me to lose my dream job and *not thinking* fractured my family, and *not thinking* made me a registered sex offender for the rest of my life. The sad truth is that I have made countless terrible and dangerous decisions in my life, but the consequences had been mostly superficial until December 2015 when I found myself in Cook County Jail facing twenty-two felony charges. It's almost as if someone or something somewhere had been storing all of the appropriate repercussions of my thoughtless, irresponsible, and birdbrained actions since I was fifteen years old and then decided to give them to me all at once when I was forty-one.

I want to make one thing clear to anyone collecting *my* story. All of my compassion, empathy, and desire to make a difference in the world sprouted first from the seeds that my mom so thoughtfully planted and watered during my childhood. And she continues to tend to that garden today. I've gotten down in the dirt myself a few times over the last five years to pull some weeds and spread some fertilizer, but all of the perennials that my mom planted years ago are still there, and they are thriving, lush, and beautiful.

This I can say with certainty: most of what makes me who I am today comes directly from my mom. I am haunted by the thought of her feeling responsible in some way for any of the bad decisions I've made in my life or for the consequences I'm facing today. And the thought of my mom blaming herself for my issues with addiction weighs heavy on my conscience every day. All she should ever do is take credit for how I've handled it, for my resilience, and for the way I've bounced back. She should pat herself on the back every morning for her role in raising a man who didn't give up after he nosedived

MY MOM

into the rocks at the bottom of his downward spiral, a man who is willing to look in the mirror and own his character defects and mistakes, a man who made the conscious decision to learn from those mistakes and to use them to get better, a man who is not too proud to evolve. And like my mom has always done, I will continue to gather knowledge and experience as much of life as I possibly can. And I will absorb everything I learn into my spirit. And I will process it and allow it to be part of me. And I will pass all of it on to my sons. And, from now on, I will think before I act. Sorry, Billy. It just makes more sense to play it safe from this point forward.

My ability to stay on my feet and maintain any kind of forward momentum over the past seven years can be directly traced to my mother's influence on my character. Without her eternal optimism, hope, encouragement, support, and occasional nagging, there is no way in hell that I would've found new purpose and true happiness in my life again. I can't count how many times she has convinced me that all was not lost. Sometimes, she doesn't even know she's doing it. I generally don't believe in shit like this, but it is truly remarkable how often I have received a text, email, or call from my mom at a most opportune time. Almost without exception, she has reached out to me in some way during the most critical moments of my journey. I don't believe that it's a matter of some motherly intuition that pushes her to check in on me; she usually has no idea how much I am struggling.

Her influence often manifests itself as an innocuous text about getting my driver's license renewed or as an email with a link to some article about Trump's most recent attack on American democracy. Sometimes, I think of it more like the universe sending me little signs, reminding me of who I am and where I came from. I received a text from my mom just as I sat down to begin writing this chapter. The universe was obviously putting a little pressure on me to get this one right. Or maybe it's not the universe at all. Maybe my dad does have some power in the great hereafter, and maybe he has decided to use his limited influence to send me a few messages when I need them the most. He never really learned how to text or email, so it makes sense that my mom is still taking care of all of his electronic correspondence.

Here's something that needs to be said because of how true it is. Without the help I got from my mom and my brother, I most certainly would've found myself in another downward spiral. And one thing I've learned through my experience in rehab and recovery is that those spirals just get wider and more intense, and the bottom only gets lower. I can't even imagine.

JESSA
MY FORMER STUDENT, MY VICTIM

Years ago, between her junior and senior years of high school, Jessa participated in a school trip to Ireland for which I was one of the teacher-chaperones, and for a short time during her senior year, she was a student in one of my English classes. Later that year, after I crossed some moral, professional, and legal lines that I had never even considered crossing before, Jessa became the victim associated with the felony sex offense I was charged with and eventually convicted of.

As I look back and try to put the pieces together, a couple of moments continue to replay in my mind. One of those moments was a conversation I had with Jessa, her grandmother, and her mom before we left on that school trip to Ireland.

I had agreed to chaperone the school trip to Ireland sometime in 2015. This trip happened every other summer, and it was the brainchild of one of my closest teacher-friends. The purpose of the trip was unique and twofold. The students would spend their first week in Ireland studying the life and work of James Joyce at a university in Dublin. Then, on the second leg of the trip, the students and chaperones would travel the country by bus, soaking in landscapes found nowhere else in the world while learning about Ireland's rich history and wonderful traditions. I chaperoned the same trip two years earlier, not long after my dad was first diagnosed with brain cancer, and I treasured the experience I had with the students and the other chaperones I was lucky enough to travel with. Almost immediately after I returned that summer, I started looking forward to seeing the green hills and rocky crags of Ireland again.

As we planned and prepared for the 2015 trip, shortly after my dad died, the two other teacher-chaperones and I conducted interviews as part of the process to choose which students we would select to travel with us that summer. This is

JESSA

when I first met Jessa, but I have no specific memories of that meeting. She must have made a positive impression, though, because she was one of the dozen or so students we eventually selected for the trip. And, if I remember correctly, there were many interesting, intelligent, and motivated students who applied to join us in Ireland that summer.

The first conversation with Jessa that I can actually remember took place in my backyard a few months after those initial interviews for the Ireland trip. It was a week or two before we embarked on our journey, and I was hosting a barbecue at my house for all of the participating students and their families. Jessa came with her mom and her grandmother. I don't recall a specific conversation I had with any of the other students and their families, but I often think about the fateful discussion I had with Jessa, her mom, and her grandmother in the backyard of the house my family and I had only recently moved into. Jessa's mom was quite concerned about how Jessa would manage her type 1 diabetes during the two weeks she was about to spend studying and traveling in Ireland.

Jessa had learned of her diabetes only a few months earlier, and the daily monitoring and managing of her blood sugar were proving to be daunting and exhausting tasks for her, to say the least. And obviously, keeping close tabs on Jessa's condition while traveling was something we needed to take very seriously. She had already been hospitalized more than once due to her blood sugar sinking too low or spiking to dangerously high levels. And, understandably, Jessa's mom wanted to meet with the chaperones so she and Jessa could explain the daily process of managing Jessa's condition. As a part of that conversation, we all decided that one of the chaperones should be in charge of checking in with Jessa to make sure she was monitoring her blood sugar regularly and continuing to treat it appropriately.

I remember being quick to volunteer to be the teacher who would look after Jessa in Ireland. It seemed like a responsibility for which I would be well-suited. I had always been that kind of teacher, the kind of teacher who students felt comfortable reaching out to when they needed help. It was my belief that whatever I lacked in expertise in literature, I more than made up for in empathy and an ability to communicate with my students more honestly and openly than the more conventional teachers they were used to.

I considered myself more of a mentor than an English teacher throughout my entire career as an educator. And I was proud to fill that role in as many ways as possible, in both of the schools in which I was lucky enough to teach. And when I look back on the decision Jessa, her mom, and I made in my backyard that day, I wonder how differently things

JESSA

would have turned out if one of the other chaperones volunteered to look after Jessa for those two weeks in Ireland. Little did I know, but that was one of the most critical moments I would ever experience, one of those moments that would have a drastic and meaningful impact on the type of person I would become and the kind of life I would live.

The agreement we made in my backyard that day, for me to be Jessa's travel nurse, for lack of a better phrase to describe the arrangement I made with her mom, gave me and Jessa something to talk about before we even left the country. I remember going over the logistics of managing her diabetes as we sat on the floor of our departure gate, waiting for the announcement that our flight to Dublin was ready to board. I enjoyed my conversations with Jessa right from the start. She stood out to me almost immediately as a not-so-typical OPRF student. There was something about her that made me want to know more. Within minutes of meeting her, I could tell that she was creative, open-minded, vulnerable, and wise to the world in a way that reminded me of the students I taught before I moved on to the wide lawns of Oak Park. It wouldn't take me long to figure out what she had in common with those Chicago public school students I still miss today.

The two communities that I was lucky enough to teach in were drastically different, but Jessa had experienced and overcome some adversity in her life that was surprisingly similar to the experiences of the students I taught in a school and community where trauma and adversity were commonplace. But some of Jessa's life experiences had left scars on her skin, and some of those scars still caused mental and emotional pain for Jessa when I first met her.

Sometime during the first two or three days of the trip, Jessa began to open up to me and share some of the trauma she had endured already in her life. Again, for better or worse, I was the type of teacher with whom students seemed to feel comfortable sharing their stories. And I was proud to be that kind of teacher. I'm still proud. But before long, it became clear that Jessa was in the midst of a personal crisis. And as the other students and teachers were dissecting the work of James Joyce and learning about the history and culture of Ireland, Jessa and I were spending more and more time together, working on getting her to a healthier place—emotionally, mentally, and physically.

My issues with personal and professional boundaries had been obvious for most of my life, and this was certainly one of the times when I was straddling that gray area between what was appropriate and inappropriate behavior as a teacher, and as a husband, for that matter. But I had been there before, countless times in my career, and I was confident that I had made a positive impact on many students' lives as a direct result of my willingness to push the boundaries a bit and to challenge the traditionally acceptable parameters of a teacher's job description. One of the glaring differences in the situation I was facing in Ireland that summer, though, was my own vulnerable and increasingly unstable mental and emotional state.

For me to effectively negotiate a tricky circumstance like the one I found myself in with Jessa, it was important for me to be healthy and stable. It was my ordinarily clear and healthy mind that had always made it possible for me to know when and where to draw the line in the previous fifteen years of my teaching career. But I was dealing with more than one personal crisis of my own when I first met Jessa. At the time, I was facing some very real issues that I had never been forced to endure or overcome in what had been, up to that point, an incredibly privileged life.

My hero-father was dead and gone, and my attempts to escape from how that made me feel were dangerously close to killing me. I needed some serious help. And that meant that I had no business trying to help anyone else manage a personal crisis of their own. But I still tried very hard to help Jessa, and I think I really was helping her for a while. There were some obvious signs that she was making progress, and it was proving to be a helpful distraction for me at the same time. The pride I felt when I helped students like Jessa, even in the smallest ways, always inspired me. It made me feel like I had a purpose, and in this case, it helped me temporarily steer my life back towards the more healthy, productive, and positive path that I had managed to stray so far from over the previous few years.

One obvious factor in my ability to maintain my own professional and moral boundaries when I first embarked on my mission to help Jessa get the help she needed was my involuntary break from cocaine while we were in Ireland. I hadn't gone more than a day or two without using cocaine for several months leading up to that trip, and I had been looking forward to the break as much as I was dreading the negative short-term withdrawal symptoms that I was sure to experience. I knew damn well at that point that I couldn't stop using cocaine on my own terms, and in the back of my head, I thought that maybe I'd come back from Ireland feeling renewed and strong again. Maybe then I'd be able to get the proper help I needed to begin my recovery from drug addiction and learn to process and cope with the loss of my father in a healthy and appropriate way. But I was in way too deep for a two-week break from cocaine to have much of an impact on my mental health.

JESSA

Almost immediately upon returning home, I jumped face-first right back into my addiction. And, as it turns out, my addiction had been doing push-ups while I was in Ireland. It had become bigger and stronger than it had ever been. But, for more than two months after we returned, I managed to keep my relationship with Jessa above board and appropriate by the standards that I had always set for myself. And I continued to see Jessa making progress and taking positive steps towards getting her life in order.

Within a week or two of our return from Ireland, I met with Jessa's guidance counselor at school, and the two of us worked together on a support plan for Jessa. She had multiple incomplete grades from previous semesters that she needed to make up to get back on track to graduate, not to mention the approaching college application deadlines she was facing. I agreed to meet with Jessa at school to help her get some of her make-up work done while I did my necessary preparation for the coming school year.

Jessa's counselor and I also discussed a plan to have Jessa meet with the school social worker more regularly once the school year started. And I pushed for Jessa to at least get an introduction to the substance abuse counselor, too, but there were some unforeseen obstacles in the way of getting her help of that nature. Also, and this certainly raised eyebrows when the news of the investigation broke, Jessa's counselor and I enrolled Jessa in a senior elective that I taught which had proven to be therapeutic for many students in the years past. On top of that, we signed Jessa up to be a student-assistant in one of my remedial-level freshman classes. She had expressed to me an interest in a career path that would allow her to make a difference in the lives of young people who, like her, hadn't always had it easy, and I figured this would be a good chance for her to do just that.

Jessa's counselor and I thought that enrolling Jessa in my senior English elective and giving her the chance to work as a student-assistant in one of my freshman classes would allow me the opportunity to keep tabs on Jessa's progress at school. But it might also give her some new purpose in the building, which might provide her with the same feeling I got from teaching. But in the end, all of that continued contact with Jessa while I sank deeper and deeper into my addiction only ended up setting the table for me to cross all of the lines I'd worked so hard to stay on the right side of for so many years.

Just two months into the new school year, in October 2015, I walked out of the double doors of OPRF for the last time on orders from the school's administration. And it wasn't long

JESSA

before the rumors of my inappropriate relationship with Jessa had already begun to spread through the student population. The same rumors were soon making their rounds through the faculty, staff, and administration. The hallways of a high school provide fertile soil for rumors—true and false—to grow and spread with amazing speed and intensity. And once the seeds of a juicy rumor have been planted, there isn't a student, teacher, parent, or well-intentioned principal who can get in its way.

Jessa was getting the stink-eye from people she didn't even know on the very day that the story was born. And once the rumor really got legs, Jessa's existence at the high school became almost unbearable. It wasn't long before the school's administration would give her a gentle nudge out of the same double doors they sent me through. Not even a week passed before Jessa was being harassed on social media for being a "homewrecker." About a week after that, someone spray-painted "whore" on the front steps of her home.

Jessa spent the last semester of her high school career at an alternative school populated by other students who didn't do well within the walls of a more conventional school. Most of them had been expelled or, at the very least, suspended from OPRF more than once. Jessa spent her final three months of high school doing busy work to earn enough online credits to graduate. The students she sat next to during that dark time knew why she was there, and it wasn't uncommon for them to make suggestive innuendos or harass her in any number of other ways. But Jessa continued to put her head down and power through. And against all odds, she graduated early and was accepted to several colleges and universities. In the end, Jessa chose a small liberal arts school in Minnesota, a few hundred miles north of Oak Park. And I can only imagine the relief she felt as she packed her bags that fall and left the environment that was becoming more and more detrimental to her pursuit of a happy, healthy, and productive life.

Ironically, when I was a kid growing up in Oak Park, I escaped to Minnesota almost every Christmas and for a few weeks each summer. And, not so coincidentally, I also fled to Minnesota to begin my recovery from drug addiction. That must explain the sense of comfort I felt when I first learned that Jessa would be heading north like I used to, to a place I knew well, to a place where most of my extended family still lives today. But as excited as I was that Jessa managed to survive all of the aftershocks and was finally headed off to college, I never stopped thinking about all the hardship she experienced as a direct result of my inability to stay on the right side of the legal, professional, and moral lines when we returned from Ireland that summer.

JESSA

Jessa made progress during her one year in Minnesota, but she never really felt comfortable there. After a couple years spent growing and evolving, Jessa met someone who made her feel happy and safe. Eventually, they moved in together. And soon, they were pregnant. They decided to move into Jessa's mom's house back in the Chicago area before the baby was born, for practical and financial reasons. This allowed Jessa and her boyfriend to continue working, and Jessa to go back to school. At the same time, they would be able to save some money on rent and childcare once their baby was born.

In many ways, this was a smart and safe plan. Maybe this was the path of Jessa's new life. She hoped to find a new path, purpose, and place for her new life. And I think that did start to happen for her there, but she needed to move on for those things to materialize.

She bounced around for the next couple of years, picking up a few more college credits and some work experience, but more importantly, Jessa was putting time and distance between herself and the trauma she had experienced. There were some new obstacles and rough patches on her new path, but Jessa continued to get better at overcoming whatever got in her way, and she always learned something new from each of her experiences. Her resilience still astounds me today.

29

MY DAD

About a year after my dad's brain tumor was first diagnosed, it was becoming clear that his days were numbered. No more surgeries. No more radiation. And the sad waiting game that we all knew was coming had arrived. Fortunately, he was able to stay at our family farm with the help of some kind and capable in-home hospice workers. They came by a few times a day, but the rest of us were on duty all night and for many of the daytime hours. I was doing my best to get up to the farm and help on the weekends, but it didn't feel like enough. In the meantime, I was operating at about 20 percent as a teacher, husband, and father. And my drug use was predictably increasing as the last drops of life were leaking slowly from my dad's body.

About a month before my dad's eventual death, I found myself standing at the door to my boss's office. I had been struggling to keep it together for my morning classes, and it hit me suddenly as I walked down the hall that day that there was no way I could continue like this. I shuffled self-consciously into his office without knocking, and I sat down across from him as he finished up some paperwork. I remember feeling spent and defeated, but I had no plan for what I was going to say to him. What I ended up saying came out easily and without much thought. A lot of that has to do with the quality of the man I was talking to.

Alex wasn't much older than I was, and he was my kind of person in every way. He was kind, sensitive, open-minded, and passionate about teaching for all of the right reasons. I was on the hiring committee the year we chose him to be our new leader. Although there were several more-than-qualified candidates, I remember thinking that Alex was exactly the kind of human being I wanted to work with and to work for in the English division. I was right about him for many reasons, but on this day, it couldn't have been clearer.

MY DAD

When my emotional meltdown was coming to an end, my face wet with tears, Alex gently interrupted me. In his usual calming tone, he just told me to stop. I looked up at him and saw tears welling up in his eyes too. Then he told me that years earlier, at the school where he got his first teaching job, he found himself in an eerily similar situation. At the time, one of his parents was clinging to life in much the same way my dad was, and Alex was having some difficulty keeping his head in the classroom while something so all-encompassing and heartbreaking was happening in his personal life. He told me that one day he just walked into his boss's office and told him what was going on, that his boss stopped him before he could finish explaining, and that he told him to go home to be with his family. His boss instructed him not to worry about lesson plans or where the time off would come from. He just told him to go home. Alex made sure to tell me that spending those last few weeks with his family was more valuable than I could ever imagine. And he wanted to give me that same gift. He told me to go to the farm, be with my dad, and not look back. He said he'd take care of everything else at school. And he did. And it made all the difference in the world. I will be forever grateful for that gift.

I don't remember even going back to my classroom that day, but I must've at least stopped in for a minute to get my stuff and tie up any loose ends. But a day later, I was at the farm with my dad and my mom. My brother and sister were getting up there as much as they could, and some of my aunts and uncles made their way to the farm to help out during those last few weeks too. My dad had a great team in place to help him, love him, and support him in the final days of his life. And there was so much love. But he was asleep for most of the time, and when he was awake, he couldn't move without help. Any moments of mental clarity were brief and infrequent. Mostly we all just took turns sitting in his room or lying in his bed with him. And all of us talked to him. This was our chance to reminisce, to apologize to him, to thank him, to tell him stories, and to say goodbye. Most of the time, he didn't say a word, but the experience was therapeutic and healing for the rest of us in so many ways.

I will never forget one particular fleeting moment of clarity that my dad experienced as I lay in bed next to him. I was all out of stories. I was just staring at the ceiling and listening to his labored breathing when it was suddenly interrupted by what sounded like my dad trying to say something. This was very rare, so I quickly turned to him and noticed that his eyes were open. I asked him what he was trying to say. He just looked right into my eyes and asked me if he was dying. I paused for a second, maybe a few, before I said yes. I

MY DAD

didn't lie to him, and I didn't try to explain it. I just said yes because it was true. I knew he heard me because he briefly shifted his focus to the ceiling and said quietly and maybe not even to me, "Fuck this, fuck this, fuck this." Then he went right back to sleep.

Those were his last words to me. So honest and so real. And so funny. I wouldn't trade them in for anything else. He had nothing else to say to me. He had been telling me he loved me for as long as I can remember. He had taught me all of the life lessons I would ever need. I had never once wished I knew how he really felt about me or my mom or my brother or my sister. What a beautiful thing it is to be able to die with nothing left unsaid.

Maybe a week or ten days later, my dad died. But he didn't go without a show that we all thought to be pretty fitting, considering how much he enjoyed fucking with the people he loved the most. In fact, on his first date with my mom, he picked up a piece of cake and brought it close to his nose before telling my mom that he thought it smelled kind of funny. Without thinking, she leaned forward to take a smell for herself, and my dad pushed her face right into the frosting. That was their first date. Well, he'd been pushing all of our faces into the cake for as long as any of us can remember. And he managed to save something big for his grand finale.

The first couple times we thought my dad died were really difficult for everyone. But the next several times he pretended to die were incredibly funny, and not just in hindsight either. We were laughing our asses off right there, huddled around his deathbed. Each time his breathing would slow, then he'd make that death rattle everyone talks about. And after a minute or two of that, he'd stop breathing altogether, sometimes for a few minutes or more. He even had the hospice nurses fooled a couple of times, and you'd think their experience watching people die for a living would've made them a little harder to fool. But when my dad would suddenly and abruptly open his mouth in a giant gasp for air, right as we were telling him to go to the light or to say hi to grandma or whatever, we'd all start laughing and hugging each other. Then we'd get ready to do it all over again. We were surrounding him on his deathbed for one final show, my dad's last chance to hold court and to make people laugh like he always loved to do. How perfect. But, in the end, he knew better than to keep this up for too long. He waited for the rest of us to leave the room, until he could be alone with my mom, to die one last time. And that says it all.

After about an hour of us all crying and laughing and raising glasses of good Italian wine to toast my dead dad, the director from the local funeral home came barreling down

MY DAD

the dirt road in his old station wagon. And after some confusion, he wheeled in the stretcher that he would eventually lift my dad onto before rolling him out and loading him into his car. I remember helping this kind of sleepy guy as he awkwardly maneuvered my dad into some kind of body bag. And as he was guiding the zipper up towards my dad's expressionless face, he turned to me and told me that he used to play golf with my dad. He said he always enjoyed it when they got paired up together. But before he closed the door of his makeshift hearse and drove off with what was left of my dad, he made sure to remind me that I was lucky to be raised by such a good man. I bet my dad never ran out of questions to ask this small-town undertaker from middle America.

There are always more stories to collect.

EPILOGUE

JESSA
A SURVIVOR, MY PARTNER

For many of the five years that have passed since my conviction, Jessa and I have managed to keep the lines of communication open between us. Sometimes, months would pass without a word from either of us, but we managed to stay in contact with each other on and off since the day the news broke. There were also stretches of time when we'd communicate daily, but we started checking in with each other a little more often once she moved back home.

She was excited and anxious about having a baby, and I was excited for her. It was clear to me that, her age and bumpy road in life aside, Jessa was as ready and prepared as anyone could be for the unavoidable challenges of parenthood. There was a new maturity in her voice and a new purpose in everything she did. But shortly after she gave birth to her healthy and beautiful daughter, it became clear that things were not going to work out with her daughter's father. In the end, they decided to break up, and he moved out.

This wasn't easy for either of them, but they remained focused on doing their best for the child they brought into the world together. Their romantic relationship was over, but they were determined to work together to provide their daughter with a comfortable and happy life filled with the love and support she deserved. And they continue to do this today. Something that many young people in their situation would have a much more difficult time managing and maintaining has been relatively smooth for them, all things considered. I truly admire both of them for how hard they have worked at it and for what caring and thoughtful co-parents they have become.

It wasn't long after this change in Jessa's relationship status that she and I decided to meet for breakfast. I vividly remember sitting in a booth and watching her struggle through the

EPILOGUE

door and into the restaurant. She was carrying her daughter in a brand-new car seat, snug against her side. The gravity of the moment was not lost on either of us. Just four years earlier, she was still in high school, and I was out on bond, facing twenty-two felony charges stemming from the legal boundaries I decided to cross. So much had changed for both of us, and there was so much more to come.

There was a strong bond between us, and while it was clear that we cared deeply about each other, there was also an undeniable complexity to the feelings we had for each other and the connection we shared. What started as an important and meaningful friendship eventually developed into a loving and committed relationship. In some ways, I think of that breakfast as our first date, but I don't think either of us thought of it that way at the time. It's hard to imagine how it all happened or how we ended up here, happy and together.

It has always been abundantly clear that Jessa and I both had a growing desire to support each other through difficult periods of our lives. Some of that desire to help each other may have been borne of guilt and shame over what happened between us and the consequences that followed. I'm sure that we continued to be drawn to each other, at least in part, through our shared traumatic experience. But whatever it was, or however it began, there is no doubt in my mind that it evolved into what can only be described as a genuine and enduring love for each other.

Believe it or not, almost exactly five years after I was put on administrative leave, never to return to the job I loved so much, Jessa and I sat down for dinner with *my* mom. About a week before that dinner, as my mom and I were driving to see a sick relative in Wisconsin, I gently broke the news to her that Jessa and I had been seeing each other for several months and that we were in love. I will never forget the way my mom's face changed when I dropped this very unexpected information on her that day, nor will I forget the difficult conversation that followed. The initial shock, fear, and anxiety my mom felt could not be disguised as anything else, despite how hard she was trying to keep an even keel and be understanding as we continued down the highway towards my aunt and uncle's farm. We talked about it all a few more times over the next couple of days, and my mom and I decided together that she needed to meet Jessa in person. Sooner rather than later. We didn't let the COVID-19 pandemic get in our way. And a few weeks after my mom and I returned from Wisconsin, we arranged for the three of us to have dinner together at a restaurant near my mom's condo in the city.

EPILOGUE

When Jessa and I arrived at the restaurant that night, my mom was waiting for us at a small table on the patio. And it was clear that she probably had a glass of wine or two to calm her nerves before we got there. "So, here we are," my mom said as she stood up to greet us. I remember there being some awkward laughter as we pulled out our chairs and sat down. My mom went on to ask Jessa dozens of questions over dinner, but the very first question she asked is one I won't forget. Seconds after Jessa and I took our seats next to each other across from my mom, she looked at Jessa and asked, "So, why do you want to do this, anyway? What is it about him?"

Jessa handled that question, along with all of my mom's follow-up questions, with honesty and grace. And I can only imagine what Jessa was thinking or how debilitating her anxiety must have been that night. But aside from looking at *me* instead of my mom as she answered many of my mom's questions, Jessa hardly seemed nervous at all. She talked openly about some of the obstacles she'd faced in her life, about her nine-month-old daughter, and about the complicated circumstances surrounding her relationship with her daughter's father. She outlined her reasons for choosing social work as a career path, and she talked about the job she was managing to hold on to while she was also attending classes and dealing with the chaos and confusion that comes along with being a new mom. It felt like I barely said a word all night, which is not normal or natural for me. But on that night, I was glad to just observe the two of them and occasionally fill some dead air with a silly comment when I got uncomfortable.

After dinner, Jessa and I walked my mom back to her condo. And I noticed a huge smile forming below my nose as Jessa and my mom shared a heartfelt hug, then stepped back to look at each other again. My mom's parting words to Jessa that night were funny and sweet. She said, "You are a wonderful girl...I mean, woman."

I hugged my mom and thanked her before Jessa and I took a deep breath and began our walk back to my car. We were a lot lighter on our feet than we were a few hours earlier when we were still carrying the anticipation and anxiety of the unknown. Jessa and I had just cleared another of the many hurdles that we'd face together. And gaining my mom's acceptance and eventual approval of our relationship was one of the hurdles we considered most important. The weight of our secret was lessening every day. And the hope we both felt continued to grow.

The five years between these two family meetings, one in my backyard years earlier and one that took place over dinner on that outdoor patio in the city, were full of self-reflection and significant life experience for me and for Jessa. While I

EPILOGUE

was stumbling my way through probation, therapy, rehab, recovery, and divorce, Jessa was just beginning to find her way in the world. She was finally putting some distance between herself and her old life and beginning to forge a new path, away from all of the chaos, sadness, and anxiety that was left in the wake of what I had done. But I will never be able to rid myself of the guilt and shame I feel for what she had to endure before she finally packed up and headed for college in the great Northwoods of Minnesota.

It has been a little more than a year since I first introduced Jessa to my mom, and since then, the three of us have met for dinner several more times. But even more meaningful and significant than that is the fact that Jessa and my mom have begun spending time together without me. And after two or three dinner dates, they seem to have moved on from talking only about what happened so many years ago. They have begun to get to know each other as people, separate and distinct from the storm I created, and they are coming to love and respect each other as their relationship continues to develop. I can't possibly explain how much this means to me.

Jessa and I have managed to clear several more important and daunting hurdles in the months following the dinner date with my mom. We resisted any urges to tell people other than my mom about our secret relationship for close to a year. We wanted to make sure that what we had was healthy, real, and lasting before we forced our loved ones to process the reality of it. So, with the guidance and support from both of our therapists, we made careful plans to start breaking the news to the other people in our lives. It was something like a soft opening of a new restaurant. We let our family and close friends in for a few meals before we opened up to the general public.

I was most concerned with telling Dana about my relationship with Jessa. Deep down, I knew that Dana would want me to be happy and that she wouldn't be upset about me finding love in a new relationship. But I also knew that learning about your former husband's new partner can be difficult and maybe even painful even in the most ideal circumstances. And I was not blind to the fact that when Dana eventually heard that I had been in a relationship with Jessa for more than a year, it was bound to open some old wounds. The last thing I wanted to do was to hurt Dana any more than I already had. But I knew I needed to be open and honest with her about this development in my life.

I convinced myself that I needed to rip the Band-Aid off carefully, but I eventually dialed Dana's number and did my best to be sensitive to her feelings as I gave her the necessary details

EPILOGUE

about my relationship with Jessa. I know it wasn't easy for her to hear what I was telling her, and I hated doing it, but Dana handled it with the emotional and intellectual maturity I only wish I possessed. We had one more polite conversation about it all a few weeks later, and our relationship as friends and co-parents has continued without any noticeable effect. The next step was to let my kids in on the secret I had been keeping from them for more than a year. I couldn't wait for Jessa to get to know them and eventually to become part of their lives.

One morning when the boys were staying with me, I woke them up with the announcement that I had made a big breakfast that I was sure they would love. And over scrambled eggs, bagels, fruit, and fresh-squeezed orange juice, I told them that I was in love. And that the person I was in love with happened to be the former student whom I once had an inappropriate relationship with while I was a teacher. I told them her name was Jessa and that she had a daughter they were sure to love. Then I filled them in on the details regarding where Jessa was going to school and what she was studying. And then I told them that she was twenty-three years old. Rocket interrupted me before I finished and said, "It doesn't matter how old she is, Daddy. Are you happy?" I assured both of my little guys that Jessa made me very happy, and I told them how excited I was for them to meet her.

When all was said and done, both of my boys seemed relatively unfazed by my big news. They even seemed excited and happy for me. I think whatever concerns they may have had faded quickly when I told them that my mom had already been spending time with Jessa and that she really liked her too.

Since breaking the big news to my sons that morning, Jessa has come over for dinner and board games a few times, and it has gone extremely well. It feels natural and comfortable. I continue to check in frequently with the boys and with Jessa as we move forward slowly. It's a tricky and unusual situation, to say the least, but the first stage of introductions has been pretty smooth. And that makes me incredibly happy.

Jessa and I manage to coordinate our complicated and busy schedules in a way that allows us to spend at least a few nights a week together. We cook for each other and go for walks. We watch *The Office* and play Backgammon. We exchange our favorite books, and we read them together. We discuss almost everything she learns as she pursues her graduate degree in social work. And we plan road trips. We talk about the silly things our kids do. Jessa teaches me about music, art, and fashion. And I teach her about addiction, poetry, and how phones used to be attached to the wall. She occasionally joins me at one of my twelve-step meetings. We go to White

EPILOGUE

Sox games and the best Chicago Blues venues...and we rarely notice the twenty-four years between our birth dates.

Sometimes, Jessa and I still talk about the difficult and painful experiences we have navigated separately and together over the last several years, but we always make sure to tell each other how grateful we are. We understand that we have lots of work ahead of us if we are going to make our relationship work and that there will be people we care about who will have a hard time accepting it. And we are painfully aware that it will not be easy. But we are convinced that it will be worth it in the end. We love each other. And, really, that is all that matters, and all that will ever matter.

ACKNOWLEDGMENTS

It would be impossible to properly express how much gratitude I have in my heart for all of the people who have supported and encouraged me throughout the process of writing *Between the Lines*. But let me start with this incomplete and inadequate attempt to do just that.

Thank you to Scribe Media and Houndstooth Press for helping me fine-tune *Between the Lines* and making it possible for me to share these stories and my own with a larger and wider audience. Your support and guidance have allowed this pipe dream of mine to have a real and lasting impact outside of my inner circle of friends and family.

And thank you to everyone else who took the time to read sections of *Between the Lines* and for providing me with the honest and sometimes heartbreaking feedback I needed. If there was any chance of me getting it right, I needed to listen to everything you had to say. I hope I didn't disappoint any of you. Most notable of these folks are Dr. G., Mo, Coryn, Carla, Marge, Chloe, and Trish. But there are so many more who showed me support and provided the necessary encouragement along the way. A million thanks to you all.

Thank you to my friends, past and present, for saving me, holding me up, and giving me hope. You know who you are. Cheers.

And I couldn't possibly create a gratitude list without including all of the human beings who shared their stories with me. Their willingness to be honest, open, and humble allowed me to create something that will undoubtedly help countless other people. Their stories will spread empathy and foster personal evolution in all who read them. Quite literally, *Between the Lines* wouldn't exist without you. Thank you for all of it.

I owe the most thanks to my family—to my cousins, aunts and uncles, and brother and sister, who love me unconditionally. And for letting me collect some of your valuable stories too. And you're welcome. It wasn't easy to leave a few doozies out of *Between the Lines* for your sake. But I reserve the right to share them in the sequel if you ever stop loving me. I kid. Kind of.

ACKNOWLEDGMENTS

And I would be remiss if I didn't take the time to thank the three most extraordinary women anyone could be lucky enough to have in their corner. My mom, my ex-wife, and my partner have been, and continue to be, the most powerful and benevolent forces in my life. These three women are responsible for almost everything in me that is good. Over the years, I've given each of them multiple opportunities to throw in the towel and leave me in the dust, but if any of them even flinched, I didn't notice it...even during the worst of times.

Despite the good intentions of the person who said it first, or of those who have quoted it over the years, the old saying about a great woman being behind every great man is demeaning, inaccurate, and flawed in more than one way. Although I am still striving to become a great man, I've had three great women in front of me, at my side, *and* behind me all the way. And I will never be able to thank them enough.

Lastly, thank you to my dad for being the perfect model of manhood.

I love you all.

www.ingramcontent.com/pod-product-compliance
Lightning Source LLC
Chambersburg PA
CBHW030442090526
44586CB00044B/516